COPING AND ADAPTING

HOW _YOU_ CAN LEARN TO COPE WITH STRESS

Dr Robert W. Howard

ANGUS & ROBERTSON PUBLISHERS

To Judith

ANGUS & ROBERTSON PUBLISHERS
London . Sydney . Melbourne

This book is copyright. Apart from any fair dealing for the
purposes of private study, research, criticism or review, as
permitted under the Copyright Act, no part may be reproduced
by any process without written permission. Inquiries should
be addressed to the publishers.

First published in Australia by Angus & Robertson Publishers in 1984
First published in the United Kingdom by Angus & Robertson (UK) Ltd in 1984

Copyright © Robert W. Howard 1984

National Library of Australia
Cataloguing-in-publication data.

Howard, Robert W. (Robert Wayne), 1953-
 Coping and adapting.

 Bibliography.
 Includes index.
 ISBN 0 207 15042 7.
 ISBN 0 207 14946 1 (pbk.).

 1. Stress (Psychology). I. Title.

158'.1

Typeset in 11 pt Baskerville
Printed in Hong Kong

Preface

This book's major aim is to help the reader better cope with the stresses and strains of daily life. The approach is twofold. Firstly, in Part I, I try to give a broad perspective on the nature of stress and the many ways people deal with it. The early chapters describe what stress is, why we experience it, and note some of the principal methods that different people use to cope with it. Part I also covers some major stress factors that we all eventually have to face and gives reasons why some people seem so much more adept at handling them than others. Part I may also be read for a better understanding of human nature, since the struggle to cope with the pressure of demanding circumstances is at the root of much human behavior.

Part II provides a set of techniques to better handle stress and to reduce the number of stressors — stress factors — one faces. These are offered, one might say, in the form of a menu from which the reader may select those best suited to his or her needs.

My hope is that this book will help in some small way, along with other works in the area, in filling a major gap in Western education. While schools and parents do their best to develop in persons many skills they will need for later life (ranging from reading and writing to driving, and so on), they often give very little explicit training in general ways to cope with life strains. Yet this is one of the most important sets of skills one can have.

Since this book is aimed at a general audience, it does not seek to summarize all or even much of what is now known in this richly researched area. The goal is to list some of the more important findings, principles, and techniques in an easy-to-follow and interesting manner.

Finally, I would like to thank here several persons who aided in the work's production, notably Dawn Cumes and Diana Yallowley for commenting on some of the chapters, and Diana Yallowley and Judith Graff for their encouragement.

50-55
90-92

Contents

Introduction

We live in a very complicated, continually changing and always uncertain world. And so, throughout our lives, we all have one overriding individual problem to solve: how to come to terms with the world, how to adjust successfully to it. In other words, how to cope with the stresses we encounter, and thrive. The stakes are high: our well-being and happiness. Somehow we must deal with a wide variety of stresses: moving to new neighborhoods and jobs, marriage, the great adjustment strain of one's first child, changes in the nature of one's marriage, in one's partner's needs and aspirations and so on. We have to cope with major life crises such as adolescence, ageing and retirement and often unexpected ones like unemployment or the loss of a loved one.

Today the sheer amount of change we face is greater than ever before. Society is itself altering rapidly. New mores, social rules and fashions come and go overnight. Tremendous advances in technology, from computers to genetic engineering, are transforming our lifestyles and work habits dramatically. Many people now migrate from country to country and have to adapt to new assumptions about life and new ways of living.

All this ferment is taking its toll. While we humans are by nature adaptable creatures, events can now move swiftly enough to strain our powers to handle them. The symptoms of this strain are all around. There is much unhappiness. Overstress, anxiety, depression, chronic anger and frustration, all symptoms of faulty coping, are widespread. Consumption of chemical remedies for these symptoms — tranquillizers and alcohol — is very high: Valium is now the most prescribed drug. Popular magazines abound with articles on dealing with stress. And, a whole host of stress-related ailments such as hypertension and heart disease are very common.

Yet, while so many cope poorly with their lot, some people still seem to thrive. They appear flexible enough to deal with shifts in lifestyle, residence or even spouse. They sail through their life crises with apparent ease and stay cool in extreme situations like natural disasters. They always seem to succeed when others either go under or adapt in ways that only keep their heads above water. Some grow and thrive, while so many others just get by.

Why is this so? What makes some good at coping when others are not? Are there ways to teach faulty copers to be good ones, and thus reduce much needless suffering? An army of behavioral scientists has been working on this and related problems for decades. Much is now known about the different ways in which people adapt to change, to new situations and to other sources of stress. The knowledge comes from studies of well-adjusted people and their traits, and from studies of people who have experienced extreme situations like war, floods and fires. It comes from laboratory experiments on stress and from a wealth of data gleaned over the years from the psychiatrist's couch.

Much of this research has pointed to a very interesting conclusion. The ability to cope well may be seen as a developed set of skills and not just something innate. Good copers know things about stress, and about themselves. They have certain mental attitudes, and they know how to and when to yield to and get used to the inevitable. Such coping skills can be learned and this book aims to suggest some ways of doing so.

PART I

CHAPTER 1

Stress, Adaptation and Coping

STRESS

Even before inventing a word for it, our caveman ancestors must have had some knowledge of stress. They must have noticed that many symptoms of arousal occurred when facing dangers like a hungry-looking sabre-tooth tiger or a marauding band of other humans. They must have realized that after several such experiences in a short time they often felt tired, malcontented, sick and unhappy (Selye, 1980).

Nowadays we have both a word for and a long list of familiar symptoms that make up this syndrome. These include feeling tense and uncomfortable, trembling, faintness, sweating, butterflies in the stomach, tight muscles, and perhaps a sense of being overwhelmed. It can range from a mild bout on a first date or when giving a brief talk to a tiny audience, to overwhelming panic in a life-threatening situation like combat or during a natural disaster.

The stress reaction can be short, like the transient grip of fear when mounting a podium or while awaiting an imminent job interview. It can hit briefly when a person faces a temporary crisis after a long period of clear sailing. Or, it can occur repeatedly over a long time. Examples are long-term imprisonment with low stimulation and separation from loved ones, difficult home or work circumstances, or deep unresolved mental conflicts. Such long-term exposure to stress can lead to many symptoms; restlessness, unhappiness, insomnia, little energy, tension headaches, and a whole host of physical ailments.

But what exactly is stress? It is quite a vague term used in many different ways. Here we stick with a fairly restricted definition favored by many stress researchers. Stress is a reaction to a demand of some sort. The demand calls upon a person to act in some way; his or her skills and knowledge must be marshalled to handle it and the outcome of the whole action is important to well-being. For example, consider a person hunting in darkest Africa who suddenly hears a roar and sees a lion about to pounce. This sound and sight creates a demand, one to do something about the situation and very soon. And the results are important: the hunter's life. As a second example, consider a person who lives in difficult domestic circumstances and often feels tense, tired and irritable because of it. Here the situation again creates a demand to do something about it so well-being will be restored.

An example of a broader set of demands is a shift in residence to a new city or country. For a time, many demands may be placed on the migrant. He or she must figure out the rules and norms of the new environment, how to meet basic needs such as security, friendship, housing and so on. The dangers of the new place must be learned about and avoided.

One can also have internal demands, internal stressors. Examples are guilt, loneliness or simply the feeling of too-few rewarding events in one's life. All these can put long-term, accumulating pressure upon a person.

According to the doyen of stress researchers, the late Hans Selye, all strong stressors produce a constellation of physical symptoms to which he gave the fancy title of the *general adaptation syndrome*, or GAS. As Selye (1980) put it, the stress reaction consists of three major stages. The first is *alarm*, the sensing of exposure to some stressful event (for example physical danger). This sets off a flow of adrenalin which mobilizes the body for action to deal with the threat. The heart speeds up, digestion slows right down, the stomach releases hydrochloric acid, and more blood flows to the muscles needed to deal with the emergency. Next comes the *resistance* stage, where the body actively tries to do something about the source of stress (for example, flees). If this phase lasts too long, or if the GAS is repeatedly elicited in a short period, the body's resources to deal with stressors become depleted. Then the third stage, *exhaustion*, may set in. In this the symptoms may be the same as during the alarm phase but the body has little power to do anything about them. Indeed, general resistance is lowered and a person may become prone to a whole host of stress-related ailments.

Recent research has suggested that the body's reaction to stressors is not anywhere near as general as Selye thought. For example, it has been shown that extreme heat produces a somewhat different constellation of responses than does extreme cold. But it still is a useful way to think about stress.

The stress reaction itself is of course programmed right into our genes, for good reasons that lie far back in our evolutionary history. For early humanity it promoted survival. The reaction was part of our defensive equipment to counter threats and other sorts of demands, a response that indeed served primitive humanity well. The world was a much more physically dangerous place then, with many predators, and other animals competing for scarce food supplies.

An extreme case of the GAS is Walter Cannon's fight/flight response. Cannon proposed it served originally as a mobilization of the body's resources to deal with an immediate life-threatening situation. Depending on the individual and situation, the stress response led to one of three major actions. One was straight flight from the source of danger, into the nearest tree, for example. Fright would almost literally lend wings to feet. Another was freezing, remaining motionless in the hope of avoiding detection. (One can see weaker versions of such reactions in everyday contemporary life. People try to flee unpleasant social situations, or freeze up in job interviews or when facing a large audience.)

The third major action was anger, which could lead not to the two F's of flight or freezing but to the third; fighting. Perhaps anger was more likely when the circumstances made it more adaptive; when cornered, or when the other fellow was smaller and weaker. Anger served as an energizer and a blocker of feelings of vulnerability, which would otherwise inhibit aggression. Many a marriage counsellor will attest to the function of anger. In the heat of a marital dispute, one partner may tell the other all his or her faults, annoying habits, personal ancestry and likely final destination in life. The fear of retribution is temporarily pushed aside and much comes out that otherwise would not.

In everyday modern life, the stress response is often

triggered off by what Richard Lazarus (1976) calls "primary appraisal". Most events in themselves are not stressful. Instead, the mind sees them as stressors, appraises them as stressful and this sets off the stress reaction. This was shown in an experiment in which groups of volunteers were told that they would get a painful injection. But while one group actually received this stressor, the other did not. Physiological signs of stress, however, occurred in both groups. They had both appraised the event in the same way. Indeed, this primary appraisal is often why certain events greatly perturb some people while leaving others unmoved. Some see a given event as a stressor but others do not. Indeed, the anticipation of a stressor can be worse than the stressor itself.

After this primary appraisal, another kind of perception comes into play, according to Lazarus. He calls it "secondary appraisal". It is a calculation of whether one's abilities and/or resources are up to the demand, whether they can handle it satisfactorily. If one feels one cannot cope, the intensity of stress symptoms may increase. The hunter, for example, might suddenly find that his rifle has jammed, or that the only tree handy is closer to the lion than it is to him. A person facing a crisis like imminent unemployment might feel even worse if he appraises his material and personal resources as not up to handling it, and if he sees his current job skills as precluding his finding other work.

In modern life, eliciting a mild stress response can be useful for several reasons. As Selye points out, stress can be the "spice of life". Mild amounts add color to life, which is one reason why horror movies, roller-coasters, skiing and motorcycling (to name but a few activities) are popular. Stress can motivate us to perform certain everyday tasks which we might otherwise not do. One example is the fear of failure which gets a student to study for an exam.

Indeed, there seem to be optimal amounts of stress for performing any particular task. If the stress level is too great, performance diminishes (for example, if too anxious in an exam or public-speaking situation). And at lower levels, there may not be enough motivation to perform well. This principle is called the Yerkes–Dodson law, and seems to apply to many different situations, occurring in animals as well. It is shown graphically in Figure 1.

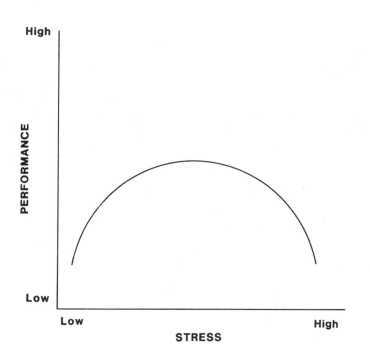

Figure 1 *The Yerkes–Dodson law. As stress increases, performance first gets better but then declines.*

But while small doses of stress are useful, the GAS nowadays is not so adaptive. The problem with it is that we have managed to eliminate most of the physical dangers that this fear/anger syndrome was designed to deal with, at least in Western nations. There are few fierce land animals left except in zoos and real danger from other people is mostly kept in check by the police and army. Yet, certain stressors may still repeatedly elicit the GAS. Consider lines of snarled traffic on the way to work, a dressing-down from the boss, the noise and pollution of major cities, a government bureaucracy resistant to one's needs, and rapid, bewildering social change. These are best dealt with by a rational problem-solving approach or by relaxation, not responses like fear and anger. The environment to which we must adapt is quite different from that of early humanity.

And besides not helping to solve many of our problems of adjustment, repeatedly eliciting the GAS may be quite harmful.

It can have bad physical side effects. The immune system which fights off micro-organisms and cancers may become weakened, leaving one more prone to a whole host of ailments. Many diseases seem to have strong stress components which can allow acute and recurrent attacks; herpes and psoriasis, for example. Other ills may take years to develop but seem closely tied to overstress. These include ulcers, heart disease, hypertension and perhaps even emphysema.

Too much stress can have many harmful psychological effects. The extreme examples of these are "nervous breakdowns" or the post-traumatic stress syndromes that we examine in Chapter 4. Others are everyday unhappiness, insomnia, anxiety, depression, onwards to what some writers refer to as existential despair. If one does not deal effectively with stress the consequences can be severe. In the worst cases suicide may be the tragic result.

ADAPTING AND COPING

Whenever we face an event we appraise as a stressor, and whether it is done successfully or not, one of two things usually happens; adaptation or coping. *Adaptation* is simply becoming used to the stressor, with no apparent effort to do so. It is a passive process which we look at in more detail soon. *Coping* is an active effort to either do something about the source of stress or to lessen its symptoms. For example, the fight/flight responses are ways of coping with certain stressors; by destroying them or getting away from them. Alcohol, on the other hand, is a way of coping with symptoms, rather than the stress source itself. Coping and adapting are hard to disentangle in many instances. In a situation like marriage or unemployment, for example, people no doubt adjust to their new circumstances through a combination of both. Let us now look more closely at each one.

Adaptation is a very useful ally in our battle to deal with the stressors of changed circumstances. It is an ally that occurs among most species in the animal kingdom. Its simplest case is what experimental psychologists call habituation, the power simply to get used to certain events over time. To illustrate, imagine someone repeatedly ringing a gong nearby. The first time it goes off, you might jump, showing a classic startle reaction. The second or third time you would probably jump less, and after a number of soundings would hardly react at all. You would have habituated to the gong.

The same basic phenomenon occurs with many events in the world. A person moving to a new house might be bothered for a while by noisy trains going past, the roar of traffic, the loud barks of the dog next door, or the flashing of nearby neon lights. But, after a while they just do not get noticed. In fact, one may become so habituated to such noises that only their absence is noticed. Once in Chicago, local police began receiving vague phone calls in the early morning hours that "something funny was going on". But the callers never seemed to pinpoint exactly what that something was. After a while, the police realized the problem. All calls came from the same area through which an extremely noisy train was no longer travelling because of revised schedules! This power to habituate evolved as a way of stopping us responding at full force to stimuli that events later proved quite harmless.

Habituation may be a case of a wider principle of adaptation, according to Joachim Wohlwill (1974). This is Harry Helson's principle of adaptation-level, used to explain how we adapt to new levels of stimulation. It is of fundamental importance and so will be described in detail.

Imagine yourself in a dark psychology laboratory with only a small, solitary light bulb in front of you. The brightness of this bulb is varied within a narrow range, different intensities being shown for about twenty seconds. After a while, you establish an *adaptation-level* somewhere in the middle of the range. This is an idea of what the "average" brightness of the lights you see is. Once it is formed, you judge the brightness of any new lights you see in relation to it. Say you are shown a medium-intensity light. It would seem quite bright to you if your adaptation-level is in the middle of à dim light range. You judge the medium one in relation to this. Now, say that you are shown a series of only very bright lights, also within a fairly narrow range. After some time, your adaptation-level would shift upwards, to stabilize somewhere in the middle of these. Say the middle-intensity light again is shown. Now it will seem dim, because it is judged in relation to a higher adaptation-level. The same experiment can be done with other variable factors, such as lifted weights, the pitch or loudness of sounds, and so on, with similar results.

The principle may account for how we become accustomed to varying degrees of stimulation. Consider a villager used all his life to peace, quiet, few people and little traffic, who moves to a large city. The city would be at the opposite end of the noise/ stimulation spectrum and because his adaptation-level is set at the other end may seem at first a noisy chaos. But, after some time the level should shift upwards and his quiet village may then seem unduly placid. People may get used to varying amounts of social change or to situations of vastly reduced stimulation (such as submarines, Antarctic research stations, and living alone after a divorce) in the same way. This adaptation-level mechanism evolved for a very good reason: it helps us to adjust to different conditions and changing circumstances.

Indeed, many people whose livelihood depends on a good understanding of human nature know the adaptation-level principle, at least intuitively. A canny real-estate agent once showed me some houses. The first four were mostly run-down, set on noisy streets and were overpriced as well, but the fifth was much better. He had aimed to send my adaptation-level for house quality downwards to make the final one seem even better than it was. Supermarkets sometimes have an overpriced brand of some product mixed in with cheaper brands. The high price may make the cheaper ones seem even cheaper than they are.

Politicians also use the technique. Often a nation's yearly budget has some harsh measures that the voters normally would find hard to swallow; say a large cutback in social spending. The voters' average adaptation-level may be set somewhere near the level of last year's spending so the politicians try to shift it. Leaks come out that the cutbacks will be truly draconian and awful. So, when the actual reductions are made known, they do not seem quite so bad because they are judged against a different adaptation-level.

A final example of its practical use is taken from the American constitutional convention near the end of the eighteenth century. Two particular plans for a system of government were being closely looked at. One was for a very powerful legislature and a weak executive more or less subject to its whims. A second plan was the present system; a congress and a president of about equal power. But many delegates found the latter notion unattractive because they had had enough of powerful executives during the days of British rule. So the group that wanted that second plan carried did a very clever thing. They proposed a third option, representing an extreme on the spectrum of executive power. There was to be a weak congress and a virtual king, elected for life, who had dictatorial powers. This shifted the delegates' adaptation-level upwards, making the previously extreme plan seem more middle-of-the-road, more like an acceptable compromise.

The adaptation-level shift has some physiological analogues. The human body can adapt well to different physical demands, just as the mind can adapt to different situations. These mechanisms allowed early humanity to spread to many very different environments; from the Amazon rainforests to Arabian deserts and Arctic icefields. A simple example is the body's response to exercise. If a person goes from a sedentary life to a weight-lifting programme, for example, the body reacts to the new physical demands by increasing muscle size and tone. Similarly, if a person goes from a life by the sea to one in rarefied Himalayan or Andean air, the lungs and heart adapt to cope with the reduced oxygen level.

As mentioned, adaptation seems to be a passive event, one that just seems to happen over time without us having to think about it, and perhaps our adjustment to many circumstances occurs mainly in this way. We may initially see a given situation as stressful, suffer some of the usual symptoms but over time become used to it. Again, the noise of the city for a rural person is one example. Another is the situation of a divorcee adapting to social isolation, which may at first seem stressful but to which adaptation may occur after a while. But simply waiting to adapt is not usually a good strategy for dealing with stress. Indeed, most people generally use one or more coping methods — active ways of dealing with stress. Adaptation may take a long time to occur, and one can suffer much in the process. As well, some sources of stress are best dealt with not by trying to get used to them but by changing them instead. And finally, many stressful situations are short-term, where long-term adaptation is a remote prospect. Examples are a temporary crisis caused by a natural disaster or a public-speaking engagement.

Coping is extremely important. Much research has

suggested that the way in which a person copes with stressors is critical to well-being. Lawrence Hinkle (1973) describes an extreme example found in a survey of the stress undergone by a group of telephone operators. One of these by most reckonings should have been a nervous wreck. Her father was an alcoholic and her mother a teenaged immigrant girl. Her early life was marked by poverty with great conflict and turmoil in the household. The father had deserted the family when she was only three and four of her brothers and sisters died as children. Raised in an orphanage after five years old and put to work as a servant at thirteen, she married a chronically ill plumber's helper at twenty-seven. He died in her arms when she was forty-four and she lived as a widow afterward. Yet, despite such a gruelling life, she had few illnesses of any sort in this time (except a few days of "nervousness" after her husband's death) and was well-liked and respected by her fellow operators. Her coping powers must indeed have been formidable.

Just why is coping so critical to one's well-being? Consider physical health first. If one copes with stress by consuming vast amounts of alcohol and other drugs, ultimately these may have a deleterious physical effect. If one copes with stress-inducing physical symptoms by denying that they are serious, diseases best detected early may wreak havoc later. For example, a woman might ignore a suspicious looking breast lump, denying it is anything at all. Tales are rife of men exercising vigorously after a mild heart attack to prove to themselves that they are really very healthy.

Next consider mental well-being. For instance, if a person continually withdraws from stress-inducing situations, unsolved problems have a way of mounting up and then hitting at full force. Other ways of coping may take an awful lot of energy to maintain. Richard Lazarus gives the example of defensively positive thinking — always looking on the bright side of events in the face of great adversity. As well, certain situations are best coped with in a particular way. Using the wrong coping methods may result in even greater stress. Cohen and Lazarus (1973) give an instance of this in a study of patients the night before the traumatic event of major surgery. Many patients fell into two groups. The *avoiders* thought little about the operation, instead distracting themselves in various ways, and not worrying. The *vigilant* actively hunted for more information about the operation, talking often about what they had to face and so on. On just about every measure looked at, from time spent in hospital to the drugs taken there, the vigilant did worse. Doing little and being cooperative was most adaptive in the hospital. But in other situations, such as a shift to a new country, being vigilant and searching for useful information may ultimately be much more adaptive than doing nothing.

Faulty coping with stress may also be implicated in the spectacular amok syndrome, a not infrequent occurrence in South-East Asian nations such as Malaysia and Indonesia. The symptoms are described in detail by Westermeyer (1982). A person about to go amok typically first withdraws from social contact for hours or days and then suddenly and brutally attacks everyone within sight. Multiple killings sometimes result. The condition may last only minutes or go on for days, until the amok person is either himself killed or somehow restrained. Then may follow a profound stupor or even coma. Upon awakening, the person is usually still somewhat withdrawn and typically has no memory of his assaults. The syndrome also occurs occasionally in Western countries. Every now and again, someone will take an axe or rifle and kill as many people as possible until killed himself.

No one is yet sure of the exact causes but according to one theory amokers may be predisposed towards bottling up anger (see Westermeyer, 1982), rather than directly responding to stress-inducing provocations. They may also be overcontrolled and rigid, and, rather than admit personal responsibility for difficulties, tend to blame them on others. When the stress builds up to a critical threshold, all defences may break down, and violence follows.

Faulty coping with stress leads more commonly in Western countries to depression, an all too frequent experience of our times. Its symptoms are a sense of hopelessness, lack of interest in many things (such as sex), slow movements, and speaking little, slowly and ponderously. In the early stages, a person may have been under great stress. Take the example of a teenage male repeatedly trying to find a girlfriend and continually being rebuffed. His early efforts may have involved searching for solutions, and doing his utmost to appear presentable and charming. But, after repeated failure, resignation and hopelessness may frequently set in. Richard Lazarus suggests this can happen in grief reactions as well. After a significant loss (as of a loved one) a person may be very agitated and highly mobilized to try to cope with this stressor. But, when these efforts seem to be of no avail, depression may occur. Depression also can be sparked off by greatly reduced social and related kinds of stimulation, this too being a stressor which needs to be actively coped with.

People under much stress usually make some sort of adjustment to the circumstances which affects how much stress will later be faced. Often this is a pattern of thinking or behavior whose purpose is defensive; to ward off danger. Because it works to some extent, because it buys some peace, a person may keep it up for years. And so it may become very resistant to change.

Let us take a couple of extreme examples first. Many of the classic mental disorders are but exaggerations of defensive coping methods that we all use. Every psychiatric hospital has at least one catatonic schizophrenic, a person so withdrawn from the world that he or she may sit curled up on a bed all day. If one arm is moved to an uncomfortable, upright position, it will stay there for hours. He or she does and says nothing, lost in some inner world. This seems a way of copping out entirely.

Another extreme one is obsessive-compulsive neurosis, most likely to occur in the middle and upper social classes. The symptoms are an endless series of repetitive rituals and/or thoughts. The victim does not want to do them but cannot seem to stop. A victim might wash his hands one hundred or two hundred times a day, or repeatedly check a front door for hours to ensure that it is locked, or count every sidewalk crack or house window while walking along a street. Everything the right hand touches the left hand might have to touch as well. A person might go through a touching sequence, repeatedly laying hands on every major object in a room. Other people may also have to adjust to such behavior. One man had a wife obsessed by cleanliness. He had to go through an elaborate cleaning and decontamination procedure before entering his house each night after work.

These rituals and obsessions often seem to be a way of warding off stress-inducing thoughts. There may be deep, unresolved conflicts which a person just cannot bear to think about, stressors a person just cannot seem to handle. With his or her time mostly taken up by rituals and obsessive thoughts, there is little room to think about them. So, a little peace is gained at quite a high price.

Another example of defensive adjustment is sometimes seen among gifted children, who have IQs in the top two to five per cent of the population. It used to be thought, after a mammoth study by Lewis Terman, that these highly intelligent youngsters tended to be models of sound adjustment and leadership. But sometimes they are not, as described by Joanne Whitmore in her book *Giftedness, Conflict and Underachievement*. Wise beyond their years, they may find classmates immature and tedious, their schoolwork unchallenging and repetitive. If not spotted early, the child may withdraw from both, and get lost in daydreams or books. Some may become very aggressive, a disruptive influence in class. A strong phobia of school can develop. Either way the adjustment to circumstances can ultimately prove disastrous for the child. He or she may drop out of formal education at the first chance, and perhaps miss out on fulfilling great potential. As well, if unable to become interested in the concerns and lives of peers, they may largely opt out of social life as well. Their social development may lag well behind.

Defensive adjustments of course are common in many spheres of everyday life. After one or two love affairs that went awry, a person may avoid close relationships. A couple not so happily married may have worked out an adjustment to each other; not spending much time or many activities together, taking separate annual holidays and so on. This may minimize the friction. Another example is the man with the obsessive-compulsive wife, mentioned earlier. He may have found the cost of going through extensive decontamination procedures less than continually battling his wife. Even animals like rats can make stereotypic adjustments. Say one carries out an experiment in which a hungry rat has to jump to one of two stands. One stand has food behind it but the other has a frightening drop into a foodless net. The rat never knows which stand has which consequence and after a while may just always choose the right-hand one. This habit becomes very resistant to change, even when the experimenter later makes it obvious which alternative has the food.

15

The problem with such defensive adjustments is that ultimately they can be very maladaptive. To be sure, many people live in impossible circumstances, ones in which the stress is horrendous, and so bizarre-appearing defensive adjustments may be, in some sense, adaptive. But in many cases this is not so. A faulty adjustment may ultimately create much stress and one can miss out on many rewards as well. Consider an agoraphobic, for example, someone who deals with problems outside the house by avoiding them and staying housebound. Anxiety is avoided but so is a great deal else. Thus enduring a little more stress and using sounder coping methods ultimately may be much more worthwhile.

Beyond coping is growth and thriving. All life has the urge to expand, to grow beyond its present size. Human empires, corporations, religions and individuals have the same property — not to stand still but to push their boundaries forward. At the individual level this means understanding the world and oneself enough to live up to potentials and capacities.

Stress can be a strong force for such growth. People often gather strength and new knowledge and skills from successfully coping with an apparently unmitigated disaster. A divorce can present new opportunities to expand one's horizons. The long-term illness of a close relative can greatly enhance one's power to deal with future stressors. Even victims of crippling accidents sometimes say that the whole experience has made them better people. The Chinese have understood this fact for centuries. The symbol for "crisis" in their writing system is a combination of two other symbols: one is for "danger", and the other "opportunity".

CHAPTER 2

Some Ways People Cope

The struggle to cope with circumstances gives rise to some truly spectacular ways of dealing with stressors. A few were mentioned in Chapter 1 but there are many others. Some of the most dramatic are exaggerations of tendencies to withdraw, to pull away from difficult situations that a person feels he or she cannot handle. A rare one is *fugue*, Latin for *flight*. People have been known to suddenly disappear from work, friends and family to be found ten or twenty years later living another life. They can have a new family and lifestyle, with no apparent memory of their earlier days. It was as though their past had simply been blotted out, erased.

Another extreme withdrawal reaction was common among women in the nineteenth century: hysteria. With no apparent warning, a sufferer might simply go blind or lose the use of both arms or legs. The symptoms seemed real; pinpricks to a paralysed limb would not be felt. Doctors would search hard but find no physical cause. And most curious of all, the victim sometimes never seemed particularly concerned: he or she would have "la belle indifférence". Apparently the symptoms would develop unconsciously as a way out of problematical situations. Unseeing eyes or paralysed legs would keep a person housebound away from the stressful world outside, for example. Hysteria can also occur with soldiers during wartime. Then the symptoms sometimes involve the limb or sense organ most concerned with their combat role. Pilots may be more likely to become blind, bombardiers to develop paralysed hands, for example.

A third spectacular but very rare withdrawal reaction is multiple personality, made famous by the book and later the film *The Three Faces of Eve*. Eve developed three (and later even more) personalities, each with its own particular character traits.

It was as though three people lived inside the same head. With this syndrome, one personality is often free-wheeling and impulsive while another is just the opposite; controlled and inhibited. This bizarre coping method may be a way of ensuring that stress-inducing thoughts do not get recognized. Instead they are seen as alien, as someone else's, or just get forgotten.

The above are some extremes of everyday coping methods. But what methods do ordinary people use to cope with the stresses and strains of daily life? "A very large number" seems to be the answer. In this chapter we look at some major ones. They are classified here according to a scheme given by Lazarus (1976). He sees two basic types of coping technique: direct-action methods and palliatives, with many subtypes within each.

DIRECT-ACTION METHODS

Lazarus sees stress as resulting from some transaction between a person and his environment. As we saw in Chapter 1, the environment places a demand upon a person. With direct-action methods, a person takes direct steps to modify that transaction in some way; for example by destroying the source of stress, fleeing from it or in a couple of other ways. Lazarus cites four classes of direct-action method.

AVOIDANCE   Here one either pulls away from or simply tries never to come in contact with a particular stressor. People learn to avoid dangerous parts of town, persons they dislike or find tedious, and stressful situations. Most species of animal use avoidance to some extent.

A difficulty may develop with this method, however, under some circumstances. The trouble with successful avoidance is that it can work too well and one may never again come into contact with the original threat. So, when the original danger has gone, a person may never find out anything valuable about it. Good avoidance is thus self-perpetuating. For example, consider a teenager who has a single bad experience on his first date and thereafter avoids all dating. The anxiety caused by such situations largely disappears because he never enters them. But, if he continues, he may never learn that dating can be positive as well.

AGGRESSION   This is the other side of the coin to avoidance; an attack on the source of stress. Threats are dealt with by trying to eliminate them, not get away from them. A person or object seen as harmful is either destroyed, injured or restricted in some way. Any society uses aggression as the final back-up means of dealing with threats to it, if not by capital punishment then at least by long-term imprisonment.

However a person may feel aggressive but find the stressor too powerful to do battle with. An example might be a timid clerk often feeling angry at his boss, or the army private getting a dressing-down from his sergeant. Aggression then may be *displaced*, transferred to a weaker target. The above private might kick a dog, for example, or a post. And aggression may even be displaced to the self.

PREPARATION   This is direct action to ensure an untroubled transaction with a future stressor. When a particular stressor is imminent, one takes many steps to prepare for it. One tries to get all the information one can about what will happen, and plans ways to act in the situation. Lazarus gives the classic example of a storm shelter against the possibility of cyclones. A study of particularly well-adjusted youngsters about to make the radical shift from high school to university showed many actively preparing for the change. They would search for information about the new problems they would face, and about the various ways they could handle them. They talked to high-school counsellors, to university students, looked through the textbooks of courses they would take, and honed up their study skills.

Preparation is also a common way of coping with job interviews, another extremely stressful situation for many. Each job has different requirements and thus interviewers look for particular traits in candidates. So, candidates may try to anticipate what questions will be asked, how best to answer them and how best to present themselves. Another variant of this method is rehearsal. Here one tries to create the stressful situation and actively goes through how to act in it, just as actors do before a play or musicians before a concert. Many politicians do this before an important press conference, for example. Their aides may hammer away with all the awkward questions that the journalists are likely to ask.

APATHY Apathy is a way of reacting to extreme, uncontrollable situations. One does nothing, has a blank uncaring state of mind when confronted with very stressful and inescapable circumstances. It is direct action in the sense that one stops transacting with the environment, one stops taking action at all.

Lazarus (1976) gives two examples, both from wartime. On a submarine hit by the enemy and about to open up to the sea there is usually no panic. The men know that there is no escape and nothing can be done and so apathy sets in. The same state occurred in soldiers in Korea trapped say, between the sea and enemy fire. There was no escape and no defence in the face of overwhelming odds. So, they did nothing, passively awaiting death or capture. Perhaps the apathy reaction evolved as a way of conserving one's energy, one's resources, just in case the situation later changed and there was an avenue along which to flee. That way one does not waste energy in a presently hopeless situation.

Apathy is very much like an advanced state of deep depression. The symptoms of the two indeed seem very similar. A deeply depressed person does very little, finds it hard to move, to initiate anything. And he or she usually says that his or her actions will have no effect on anything anyway. Indeed, one prominent theory of depression says that the most common type is due to *learned helplessness*. A person comes to think that he or she is helpless (usually erroneously), that there is nothing to be done to affect the world.

PALLIATIVES

Much of the time any direct action to change a stressful situation or solve a tricky problem is impossible, doomed to fail or is self-defeating. This can be true of many events; a close friend or relative may die, a lover finally take off, one could face a spell in an escape-proof prison, or have to endure voluntary poverty and hard work while finishing off a course or degree. Even as I write, I am constantly reminded of the inevitability of some such stressors. Fifty metres down the hill from my home, work is in progress on a new block of apartments. The workers have carved out much of what was a beautifully bushed hill. They start noisily about 6.30 a.m. and go on till late afternoon. Like most other locals, I fought hard to stop construction going ahead. But, when all had failed, other than active sabotage, there was nothing more to be done. Not wanting to move, like everyone else I just had to put up with the situation.

What sort of coping method is often used in such circumstances? Some kind of *palliative*, a soother, an anaesthetic. Palliatives do not try to affect the stressful event itself, they change the way one's mind and body react and so try to ease the symptoms of stress. One continues to transact with the environment but tries to palliate the distress that certain aspects of it cause.

Traditionally, humanity has used a very wide variety of palliatives. For many people, the first line of defence against stress is chemical. Some drugs change our physical state; reduce anxiety and depression, drown out haunting memories or alter reactions to situations. Alcohol, opiates and Valium make many a difficult situation temporarily easier to face. During periods of high unemployment, drug and alcohol use tend to skyrocket as many look for relief from the boredom, money worries and blows to self-esteem that go along with it.

Another popular palliative is fantasy. Nowadays, publishers of fiction say that many readers are looking for escape so fantasy, science fiction, and romances often top the bestseller lists. Such books can allow the reader to project into a much more interesting, simpler and more controllable world, a good place to spend a few hours. Movies have a similar function, which is why Hollywood used to be called the "dream factory". And most of us sometimes retreat into daydreams, older people especially.

One that humanity has had almost since the dawn of our race is religion. Just about every human culture has come up with a supernatural system of belief, a faith. A sincere belief in a religion is indeed a great boon. It usually gives a ready-made network of people who share one's beliefs and reinforce them, at the place of worship and in other activities. It gives a reason for our lives on earth, answering the age-old question of why we are here. Most great faiths give the promise of an eternal, blissful afterlife once the pain of present existence is done. A faith provides the comforting thought that a just-departed loved one has gone to a better plane of existence and that we will eventually join him or her there. That eases the torment. Many people become very religious in the face of extreme stress; the soldier's "fox-hole conversion".

Karl Marx summarized well this function of religion in his oft-quoted remark, "Religion is the opiate of the masses". He did not mean an "opiate" only in the sense of an addictive agent that ultimately destroys the user. He meant an opiate more in the nineteenth-century sense (when heroin was seen as a good cough medicine), as a soothing, pain-reducing balm that made the struggle of life easier for the ordinary man and woman to bear.

Secular ideologies can serve the same role, though not with quite the authority that a supernatural one can lend. Some people embrace systems such as Marxism, existentialism, psychoanalysis, or even ways of better relating to others (such as transactional analysis and Gestalt therapy) with a great fervor. These can provide new understanding of the world, a way to think and talk about it, a way to answer some of its important questions.

Even a single, simple (and wrong) idea can have a great palliative role. It can reduce the complexity of the world and one's own problems to utter simplicity in one fell swoop. Adolf Hitler was able to convince much of the German population that most of the world's ills were due to the Jews. Once this race was gone, life would be simple, prosperous and easy. Many rigid thinkers have other such villains, from world Communism and sexual permissiveness to Satan.

Humor is another important palliative. A good way to make difficult situations easier to bear is to find a lighter side to them.

Another important set of palliatives is the many folk-sayings aimed at helping us cope. We or someone else may repeat them to get through some temporary adversity. Here are a few:

1. Every dark cloud has a silver lining.
2. All good things must come to an end.
3. Count your blessings.
4. It's all for the best in the end.
5. It was going to happen eventually anyway.
6. Always look on the bright side.
7. The Lord moves in mysterious ways.

DEFENCE MECHANISMS Some decades ago, a charismatic man came to believe that the world was about to end. He even knew the exact time of its destruction, but he and a select few would be saved by aliens from outer space, who would pluck them into safety in a flying saucer just before its demise. The man was persuasive and convinced a large group of others that his story was true. They duly sold their houses and belongings and waited at the appointed time on a mountain top for rescue. But the UFO never appeared that night, nor did the world end the next day. Even so, in the face of overwhelming evidence of their gullibility, few of them had any trouble coping. They did some mental gymnastics, and concluded that because of their strong faith, the planet had been saved.

The tale illustrates a quite pervasive class of mental palliatives that we all use to some extent: defence mechanisms. Here we perform some fancy thinking to bend our view of events, to look at things in a different way, or just to select out aspects that we wish to believe. This way we defend against stressful, anxiety-provoking thoughts. Many of these mechanisms were first described by Sigmund Freud around the turn of the century after he saw his Viennese patients using them. One way to look at them is as affecting one's appraisal of stressors. Either one does not see particular stressors, looks at only their non-stressful aspects, or changes one's appraisal of them from stressor to non-stressor. Let us look at some major ones in turn.

Repression This one is very common, all of us no doubt using it at times. Here one simply forgets, or *represses*, events and facts that one would prefer not to remember. Thus, most awkward social blunders, bad experiences, and not-so-great personal character traits get conveniently blotted out with time. This seems to be a basic human trait. We tend to remember the positive and good and forget the negative and bad. Often one notices this after coming back from a holiday in which everything went wrong. The hotels were shoddy, the planes late, the service grumpy and the people met none too friendly. But somehow, a few months later mostly just the good aspects are recalled. By then, all in all, it seemed like a good vacation.

Repression seems very useful for smoothing over stress-inducing thoughts and memories. But, as with most things, it can be used to excess. As Lazarus points out, a person who conveniently forgets too much may diminish contact with reality. Such a person can seem very out-of-touch, very naive. And reality often has a way of forcing us to come to terms with it. As a sage once said, "Every now and again reality takes us in for an illusionectomy".

Detachment   Here a person tries to deal with a stressor from a detached, non-involved standpoint, freeing him or herself from any emotional connection with the situation. A person says "I don't care" or "It is not my problem". Doctors and nurses learn early not to get too close to their patients because the emotional strain otherwise would become overwhelming. A prostitute unhappy with her profession may detach herself from any genuine emotional involvement with customers. She may decide she is really two people, the "real me" and the "someone else who goes out to work".

Sublimation   This one, described in detail by Freud, can be quite healthy. When a particular path seems impossible to take, a certain goal too hard to achieve, one abandons it and puts energy into attaining another, perhaps distantly related one. One therefore sublimates one goal in favor of another, not wasting time and energy in a fruitless exercise. For example, many parents who have not quite made their high childhood expectations of success in life come true may take great pleasure in their children's accomplishments instead. A person who through lack of ability fails medical school may direct his energy toward succeeding in the business world instead. A person who fails as a writer may compensate by becoming an excellent husband or wife.

Sublimation can be a problem, however, when one gives up too soon on a necessary goal and substitutes a maladaptive one. One example is sex. A person may give up hopes of a normal healthy sex life (for any one of many reasons) and seek refuge instead in pornography or voyeurism.

Denial   This one is very common. Here a person simply denies, often in the face of overwhelming contrary evidence, the existence of some discomforting fact. Parents of a child about to die from leukaemia, for example, may sit planning out his high school and university education from the hospital waiting room. People confronted with evidence of the risks of riding motorcycles, smoking, hang-gliding or overeating may either deny the evidence altogether or say "yes, but it will never happen to me". In the early stages of a natural disaster such as a flood, many people deny there is any danger to them or even that there is a disaster at all. Families of far-gone alcoholics may resist strongly the idea of any problem, saying that the person in question drinks only as much as anyone else.

Freud himself described a more extreme case: a young woman in love with a frequent visitor whom she thought came to see her. But in fact, he had been using her to see another girl in the same household and when that relationship ended ceased coming altogether. Eventually, however, she began to imagine him always there with her, denying the whole unhappy sequence of later events.

The above examples give cases where denial is mostly maladaptive. But often it is not; it can be an adaptive reducer of stress. In some instances of disasters or significant losses, denial may help a person weather the initial trauma.

Rationalization This is a thinking person's defence mechanism, of which the famed "sour grapes" syndrome is an instance. Here a person explains away, rationalizes away, any stress-inducing thoughts or inconvenient facts. For example, students doing badly in an exam may tell themselves that the test was unfair, or that they could have done much better if they had felt inclined to study harder, or even that exams are unimportant. A continually rejected suitor might tell himself that the girl was too young or too dumb to really appreciate his fine qualities. Thus self-esteem is preserved.

Projection Here a person deals with unacceptable, stress-inducing thoughts by ascribing them to others. A person particularly hostile to others might tell himself that everyone is hostile to *him*. A man might deal with unacceptable (to him) homosexual feelings by seeing many others as homosexuals.

A classic study of projection was carried out by Sears (1936). He had men in a college fraternity house rate themselves and each other on four traits: stinginess, obstinacy, disorderliness and bashfulness. Some persons who rated themselves low, and others high, on these qualities were often rated high on them by their fraternity brothers. They had little awareness of the traits in themselves.

Reaction formation Here a person has an unacceptable thought or impulse and does his or her best to think or act just the opposite. Shakespeare immortalized this mechanism with his oft-quoted comment, "Methinks the lady doth protest too much". A well-known case was a man who always appeared to be feverishly concerned with his children's welfare. He would phone his wife many times a day to make sure no harm had befallen them, and expend much effort and profess much concern on their behalf. Even the children's school received daily calls to check their safety. As it turned out, all this effort was due to quite hostile but unconscious feelings he had towards them.

Selective perception Here one only takes note of certain aspects of situations, the positive ones, and ignores all other aspects entirely. A smoker confronted with much evidence of his habit's bad effects on health may just think about its positive effects (it relaxes me) or about his Uncle Ned who goes through five packs a day and is nearing ninety years of age.

This kind of self-delusion does not seem to be an exclusively human trait. An experimenter studying animal learning assures us that the following is a true story. A monkey was trained to press a bar when a light was off. When the light was off and the room dark, pressing the bar produced food. But bar-pressing did not produce food when the light was on. At first the animal learned quickly, pressing the bar only when the room was dark. But after a while, something strange happened. The animal began to press a great deal even when the light was on. The puzzled researcher eventually took a look inside the room to see what was going on. The animal was cleverly sheltering himself from reality. When the light was on, he had one hand on the bar pressing away and the other firmly clamped over his eyes to shut out the light!

Identification This one can occur when a person is more-or-less powerless and at the mercy of some aggressor. The victim identifies with the persecutor, taking on his characteristics and behavior. Anna Freud gave an example of a little girl afraid of ghosts and therefore reluctant to cross a dark hall. So she began to make odd, spooky gestures as she ran across it, advising her brother not to be afraid, and "just pretend to be the ghost that might meet you".

Oppressed peoples may take on some characteristics of their oppressors. Kenneth Clark said that many blacks in America used to try hard to look and behave like whites, straightening their hair and bleaching their skin, and adopting whites' condescending attitudes toward blacks. Psychoanalysts also say that people who have just lost a significant loved one may strongly identify with him or her, at least for a time.

Finding meaning in adversity   Another human coping method is finding some meaning, some reason for even the worst of events. People learn to see reasons for the most senseless, difficult and capricious of circumstances. One extremely wrongheaded example comes from after the end of World War II, when some German citizens were taken through a concentration camp to see the horrors of what had been done there. One was overheard to remark to another that the Jews must have done something very dire and evil indeed to earn such treatment.

On the positive side, Silver and Wortman (1980) point out that many people suffering a major crisis keep thinking about it over and over again, trying to find some meaning, some reason for it. They cite studies of parents suffering the misfortune of a child dying from some disease as looking at the situation more broadly, perhaps seeing that what doctors learn from their child's case may help other sick children. Patients in a burn ward may see themselves as having survived trial by fire, having improved themselves by living through it. People struck down by a disease or severe accident may even appear to welcome it, seeing it as punishment for past sins which they can now be free of.

Dehumanization   This mechanism may be used when a person has to do immoral or unpleasant things to other people, usually upon orders from superiors. It can happen in wartime for example, where soldiers have to kill enemy soldiers, or drop bombs upon civilians, or take part in atrocities such as My Lai in Vietnam or the countless others of earlier wars. Here a person considers the victims not as human beings but as objects, thinking of them as bodies or numbers. That makes them easier to deal with. As a result, the moral qualms most of us are socialized to feel get pushed into the background. Getting people to use this mechanism usually takes much time. Soldiers have to be extensively trained to learn instant obedience to orders. Otherwise they might not shoot at all.

This mechanism might also provide one way for torturers working in the service of a police state government to carry on. Victims often say that their persecutors were not sadistic monsters but typical family men just carrying out what they saw as their job. They just followed orders.

As mentioned above, all of us use defence mechanisms to some extent. They seem necessary to avoid much unnecessary stress. Indeed, problems may arise when their normal use somehow goes awry. For example, a person bothered by persistent stressful thoughts or memories may for some reason have had the repression mechanism bypassed. But many disorders are but exaggerations of defence mechanisms, ones that are used to too great an extent. Obsessive-compulsive neurosis as described in Chapter 1, for instance, is an exaggeration of such everyday superstition mechanisms as actors saying "break a leg" before a play to ward off disaster, or someone saying "touch wood" when arguing that a particular stressor will not occur.

ON THE USE OF COPING METHODS

The above list gives some examples of the ways people cope with circumstances. Further methods and examples of the use of a few of them are given in Chapter 4. One might now ask which methods of coping work best in which situations, and what methods people typically use in which situations.

There is as yet too little information on these questions. Once again different people are likely to find different methods appropriate to their needs, abilities and morals. These methods may also change over time and stressors. A couple of recent studies shed some light on them.

A large-scale one was carried out by Pearlin and Schooler (1978). They interviewed 2300 adults in Chicago. They found that men, the better educated, and the wealthier were more likely to use coping mechanisms that worked efficiently. They found people using a variety of different mechanisms at different times to cope with different stressors. Interestingly, they found that coping methods were most likely to be useful in home-type situations, when dealing with problems in marriage and child-rearing and much less so in impersonal work problems.

Another study was carried out by Folkman and Lazarus (1980). They surveyed the coping behaviors of one hundred

28

ordinary middle-aged Americans, interviewing each one every month for a year. They found that the sample tended to favor direct-action problem-solving methods to deal with stressors, as well as a palliative at the same time. This occurred in something like ninety-eight per cent of the average thirteen monthly stress episodes reported by each person. They also reported using direct-action methods when they felt there was something to be done and palliatives when they saw action as futile. In addition, they did not seem to rely on just one or two coping methods. They applied different ones to different types of stressors. Stress at work might be handled very differently from stress at home, for example.

CHAPTER 3

Some Sources of Stress

Having defined stress and having covered some ways people cope with it, we can now look at some major sources of it. The potential list is of course enormous and so only a few can be mentioned here. Many of the ones examined are those that we all have to face and come to terms with, such as ageing and loss. Others like migration and crowding are not so inevitable but still may affect many of us.

First, one might ask what makes a particular event a stressor. Some events become stress-inducing because of the personal meanings they acquire via the appraisal process described in Chapter 1. Other events are stressors simply because of our biological makeup. Examples are extreme heat and cold, loud noise, lack of sleep, poor diet, body damage caused by burns and so on.

An interesting factor that can much affect how stressful such events are is their potential controllability. Generally, if one sees oneself as having control or at least the chance of control over a stressor, it seems much less potent. For example, say that a noisy party is going on next door in the small hours of the morning. The noise may not seem too bad at all if one feels able to go over and get the neighbors to turn down the music. It is easy to demonstrate this effect in the laboratory (Miller, 1980). For instance, in some experiments subjects are put to work doing some task while unpleasant loud noises sound every now and again. One group is given a button which they are told will turn off the noise if they cannot bear it. Another group gets no such button. In practice the button very rarely gets pressed, yet the group that has it there is much less affected by the noise. Just the fact of having that potential control (even if it is never used) seems to greatly reduce the stress produced by the noise.

There are many possible ways to classify stressors. The scheme we use here is one offered by Lazarus and Cohen (1976). It divides stress sources into three categories; cataclysmic, daily hassles and changes. We also describe here some major stress periods in the life cycle, such times as adolescence and retirement. While these could be classified as changes, they are important enough to merit their own section.

CATACLYSMIC SOURCES

These are overwhelming disaster-scale events which create great stress for large numbers of people at the one time. Examples are such things as hurricanes, floods and earthquakes or the depredations of war such as invasion or enemy bombing. They may create extreme situations where life, limb, family and property are at grave risk. Because they are such strong stressors, virtually everyone is likely to appraise them as such. Some major cataclysmic sources and some ways people cope with them are covered in detail in Chapter 4. Here is a detailed example of a more commonplace one.

UNEMPLOYMENT High levels of joblessness have character-ized recent times and according to many predictions will continue long into the future. Chronic unemployment can have a very severe effect upon an individual, the loss of the job itself being just one aspect. A host of others go with it.

The most obvious is a likely descent into poverty, or at least a severely curtailed standard of living. Jahoda (1979) has listed some other stressors and reactions, drawing partly from a set of studies of the unemployed in the 1930s Great Depression.

One is a great loss of self-esteem, of self-respect. Often we largely define who we are by the work we do. Our job gives us a role, a place in society. It is the source of much of our prestige. Unemployment may alter the male breadwinner's place in the family. His wife may compare him unfavorably with those still working and blame him, rather than the prevailing economic conditions, for lacking a job. Indeed, many jobless themselves do this, becoming demoralized and seeing the fault as their own. They may sink into apathy and despair with time, especially after repeated failures to find another job.

31

Another problem noted by Jahoda is the resultant amount of free time. At the start this may seem a boon but after a while many unemployed people may do less and less leisure-type activities. Work also puts us in contact with others sharing a similar experience, linking us to goals and purposes beyond our own. Freud once said that "Work is man's strongest tie to reality".

DAILY HASSLES

These are all the everyday, common or garden variety stressors. They occur, as Lazarus and Cohen note, again and again. Examples are noisy neighbors, personal conflicts at home and work, poor health, overcrowding, too much pressure at work (say through too fast a pace or too much responsibility) and so on. Others include dealing with aged parents, role conflicts (for example, with one's spouse over who should do what), environmental pollution and overactive children. Even the lack of enough positive rewards in one's life can be such a stressor. Let us look in detail at some common ones.

POVERTY No one who has been poor for any length of time needs reminding what a daily struggle life can be. There is constant concern over whether ends will meet, what one must go without this week in order to pay for some necessity. As author Somerset Maugham put it, "There is nothing so degrading as the constant anxiety about one's means of livelihood ... Money is like a sixth sense without which you cannot make use of the other five." George Orwell's novels often had poverty as a theme. One was mainly constructed around this idea, *Keep the Aspidistra Flying*. The hero decided to opt out of the "money culture" as much as he could, taking a low-paying job and living in grim surroundings as a matter of principle. The book depicts well the stresses he had to endure as a result. Nowadays, many people enter the world of poverty through unemployment, or by overusing their credit cards, buying more than they can really afford and wondering each month how to meet the ever-mounting bills.

Poverty usually means having to endure many more stressors. A person is likely to live in substandard housing with more noise and overcrowding, to live in more dangerous neighborhoods, to have less resources to tackle major stressors. For instance, a poor person usually does not have the money to take weekends away or annual overseas vacations, an important restorer of mental well-being for many. And one may have to take much superciliousness or even abuse from overzealous social-security officers.

As well, certain life events tend to pack a much greater punch when a person is impoverished. A broken appliance, a car that needs repairs, a rise in rent or some hospital bills may signal a major disaster. A better-off person would be likely to shrug them off. And poor people usually have less of a sense of control over their lives.

The link between poverty and symptoms of stress has been shown by a variety of studies. One by Ilfield (1977) of persons living in the Chicago area found that the percentage of people with stress symptoms went up as the income level went down. Another study by Myers, Lindenthal and Pepper (1973) surveyed 720 households in New Haven, Connecticut, and found that poorer people faced more stressful life events.

Some social scientists have even argued that poverty creates its own culture, its own ways of thinking and acting. These are supposed to be universal, occurring wherever poverty is found. Its symptoms include fatalism, feeling inferior, having low self-esteem, and staying locked in the present. One never thinks much beyond one's daily needs, never peers into the future to see where one is going, never makes long-term investments of time or energy. Poverty thus gives a design for living, one which is incompatible with the steps needed to lift oneself into the middle class (more education, for example). So the culture perpetuates itself.

POOR SOCIAL SKILLS Unless a hermit or lighthouse keeper, we usually face many daily interactions; with friends, relatives, workmates, teachers, superiors, lovers and so on, and even the familiar strangers at the bus stop or railway station. Our success in life largely depends on how skilfully we carry out these interactions, whether we can get what we want and need from them and whether our effect on others is positive. This power to deal well with others is a skill, one that we spend much time learning.

A person with poor social skills is likely to find many interactions painful, aversive, difficult and embarrassing. And his or her faulty skills can create a variety of bad atmospheres in places like work and so on. The constant friction of poor relationships may be a great stressor. As well, a person may miss out on many of the rewards that good human relationships can give. This topic is described in much greater detail in Chapter 5.

Closely related to the above stressor is poor communication skills. This means not being able to clearly communicate one's wishes, needs and emotions to others and to pick up their return communications. Failure to do either can lead to much misunderstanding, embarrassment and so on, as many a marriage counsellor will confirm.

CROWDING All of us need a certain measure of people-free space in which to live and move. Too little of it, too much crowding, seems to be a universal stressor. Humans do, however, seem to differ in just how much is needed. Residents of crammed-to-capacity cities like Hong Kong make do with little and may even rent out their extra space to others.

But too dense packing can have harmful effects. Some dramatic demonstrations of this were provided by some fascinating research with animals by J. B. Calhoun in the early 1960s. Calhoun greatly overpopulated an enclosed space with rats, continually adding new ones to keep up the numbers when others died. When the population density was very high, the usually tight social organization of the rats disintegrated and they began to show very abnormal behavior. Aggression was rife, infant mortality was high, and strange sexual behavior and even cannibalism occurred. Maternal care often went haywire as well, mothers abandoning their young.

Studies have suggested that overcrowding can have harmful effects on humans too. It has been linked to poor health and to anti-social behavior. Areas of high density are more likely to have higher crime rates. Such high density may also lead people to withdraw from each other to a large extent. This can be shown in miniature in an experiment; for example by filling a room with people and seeing what happens. Generally, as the crowding goes up, people tend to interact less in such a situation and look at each other less. Males also can become more aggressive and competitive when the room is filled wall-to-wall with other males.

Finally, there are different types of overcrowding and these seem to make a difference to the perceived stress. One can live in a too-densely packed suburb, a too-crowded household, or just face the daily pressure of leaving a spacious mansion to fight through city crowds. Eric Sundron distinguishes between our primary and secondary environments. The primary one is our home-base or workplace, where we spend most of our time. The secondary one is everywhere else we go; the streets, sidewalks, movie theatres and restaurants, for example. Apparently, being crowded in the primary space is more serious for many people. It seems that as long as we have some private, uncrowded place in which to recuperate, the city crowds are much easier to weather.

BEING LOW IN THE PECKING ORDER Watching monkeys together at the zoo or chickens in a yard can be very entertaining. Like many other social animals, both species form strong and quite rigid hierarchies, usually ranging from the largest and fiercest male down to the most sickly and weak. This male pecking order determines who gets what; who gets food first and who gets the scraps left over, who gets first choice of mates, and so on. The weaker animals also spend much effort staying clear of the larger ones. A top monkey can stride about the cage, going much where he pleases, while his subordinates will jump out of his way as he approaches. The hierarchy is therefore maintained by the lower ranks. The top ones usually settle who is boss by a single fight at the start, if necessary, and then need do little more. The weaker animals keep their place, not needing to be brought back into line. Some may stay restricted to a tiny corner, rarely straying outside.

We humans form hierarchies as well of course, which often seem much like those of chickens and monkeys. Large organizations have clear lines of authority, radiating from the Chairman of the Board and President (or Department Head) down to the lowliest mail-room clerk. Peer groups also often form social hierarchies, ranging, for example, from the best-dressed (or fiercest in the case of a neighborhood gang), best-looking, most socially skilled down to those at the bottom with few such valued traits. Those in the lower rungs also tend to maintain the hierarchy. In a corporation for example, often the up-and-coming will expend much effort to defer to and support their bosses. Their promotion prospects, salary and indeed whether they keep the job at all may hinge on all this.

Being low on the hierarchy is usually much more stressful than being near the top, despite the latter's added responsibility. One has less access to material resources, more of a sense of powerlessness. One must also defer to and try to understand and anticipate one's superiors' wants and reactions. One must keep out of their way at times. One must submit to occasional dressings-down, whether deserved or not. This can be seen just by watching the different postures of superiors and subordinates at a meeting. The subordinates usually have much more tense postures, watch their words carefully, and concentrate on appearing attentive and supporting. The superiors generally look much more relaxed. They may lean back occasionally, hands behind head. These behavior differences may reflect the different amounts of stress they are experiencing.

STIMULUS UNDER- AND OVERLOAD   The Pink Floyd movie *The Wall* has a long series of ever-changing, bizarre images. The scenes flick quickly from one to another, and the constant change gives many watchers an acute case of stimulus overload. They are bombarded with too many complex and at times unpleasant stimuli to take in at one time, and the experience can be quite a stressor. The opposite end of this spectrum is stimulus underload, also sometimes a great stressor. Here the environment does not change enough. There is not enough variety/flux/variation in the patterns encountered. Such underload can occur in prisons, Antarctic research stations, and spacecraft, where nothing much ever happens. Many a housewife stranded in the suburbs also may endure a similar lack of variety during the day. Another type of stimulus underload is social isolation, too little contact with other human beings. The latter can also be stressful and can lead to a variety of symptoms covered in Chapter 5.

The dramatic effects of severe stimulus underload were shown in some startling experiments begun in the 1950s. Volunteer subjects were exposed to different levels of monotony. Some were left in a blank, featureless room lying on a bed for many hours, hands and feet covered to reduce stimulation from them. Others were actually suspended in a water tank (hooked up to a breathing apparatus) to further reduce sensation. The results were astounding. Most subjects could only last a couple of days. They reported feelings of unreality, and hallucinations. One subject, for example, said that he saw a "procession of squirrels with sacks over their shoulders marching purposely across a snow field and out of the field of vision". Another said, "The whole room was undulating, swirling ... you were going all over the fool place at first ..." While not everyone doing research in this area has found such dramatic effects, these studies do suggest that we need some minimum level of stimulation to keep balanced. Many explorers and lone yachtsmen echo this belief.

Indeed, there seems to be an optimum level of stimulus change for each of us. Too little is stressful and too much is stressful. Again there seem to be wide individual differences in regard to the optimum point. Some people need a lot of change and become mountain climbers, sky divers, and perhaps mercenaries. Others need much less, and may become hermits, recluses or factory workers quite content to bask in the unvarying security of the assembly line. Nevertheless, despite being happy at an optimum point, we can usually successfully adapt to different amounts of change, as Joachim Wohlwill (1974) and others have pointed out. A study of Norwegian men (mentioned by Wohlwill) who had been living as virtual hermits found them much less bothered by sensory deprivation experiments, for example. Another study he cites found prisoners to be not unduly disturbed by a week of solitary confinement. Their overall stimulus change adaptation-level had already shifted radically downward because of their imprisonment.

We seem to be able to adapt well to overload as well, especially to the overstimulation given by crowds, traffic and pollutants in the big city. The biologist René Dubos in 1965 noted that:

Millions upon millions of human beings are so well-adjusted to the urban and industrial environment that they no longer mind the stench of automobile exhausts, or the ugliness generated by the urban sprawl; they regard it as normal to be trapped in automobile traffic, to spend much of a sunny afternoon on concrete highways among the dreariness of anonymous and amorphous streams of motor cars. Life in the modern city has become a symbol of the fact that man can become adapted to starless skies, treeless avenues, shapeless buildings, tasteless bread, joyless celebrations, spiritless pleasures — to a life without reverence for the past, love for the present or hope for the future.

Stanley Milgram wrote an interesting article in *Science* in 1970 on the ways that people adapt to the stimulus overload of the large city. He points out that the overload comes from many sources; crowds, the rush for facilities, abuse from others and so on. Milgram quotes the following:

When I first came to New York it seemed like a nightmare. As soon as I got off the train at Grand Central I was caught up in pushing, shoving crowds on 42nd street. Sometimes people bumped into me without apology; what really frightened me was to see two people literally engaged in combat for possession of a cab. Why were they so rushed? Even drunks on the street were bypassed without a glance. People didn't seem to care about each other at all.

Milgram argues that this typical big-city behavior arises from people trying to filter out the many inputs that are otherwise too overstimulating to cope with. Since city-dwellers come into contact with many people during the day, they keep balanced by becoming acquainted with many fewer than do their rural cousins, and they keep much more superficial relationships as well. People simply disregard many inputs, such as the drunk lying on the road.

MENTAL CONFLICTS   These are another cause of much of the stress of life. A conflict arises when one must choose between two or more alternatives of somewhat equal merit. They can be fairly trivial ones like where to go to dinner, what type of car to buy and who to take to lunch, or more serious ones like whether to continue a marriage or seek a better job, or conflicts between one's upbringing and current lifestyle. And many suffer a continuous battle between a need for security and stability and for adventure and change.

Conflicts come in several varieties, described by Miller and Lewin (see Mahl, 1971). First is the approach–approach conflict, where one has to choose between two quite attractive alternatives. For example, it could be which of two cars to buy, which of two people to marry, and so on. Second is the approach–avoidance conflict, where a goal has positive attractive qualities that pull one toward it but negative ones which push one away. For example, a painfully shy young man might have one on seeing an especially beautiful girl, or a previously faithful husband upon contemplating an affair. One made much of by psychoanalysts is the desire for but fear of intimacy with others. Another might be the wish to get a painful but necessary confrontation over with, linking with the fear of conflict. Third is the avoidance–avoidance conflict, where one must choose between two unpalatable alternatives. For example, a youngster induced by peer pressure to jump off a high dive has to choose between the terror of diving and the pain of losing much face if he climbs down. The folk phrase "caught between the devil and the deep blue" sums it up well.

Neal Miller has shown that approach and/or avoidance tendencies get stronger as one gets closer to the goal. The shy young man would be likely to become both more anxious and more attracted as he got closer to the girl, for example.

When the conflict is too strong, such as when the outcome is very important to our well-being or the tendencies are very powerful, much distress can arise. This was shown in an early experiment by Ivan Pavlov with dogs. He created "neurotic" animals by giving them an insoluble task. They were first conditioned to salivate to a circle but not to an ellipse. All was well and fine, but then the circle was made steadily more elliptical and the ellipse steadily more circular. The result was a highly disturbed animal, striving to make what had become an impossible discrimination.

Conflicts, when not resolved, can also lead to severe frustration, another common symptom of our times. One's avoidance tendencies can be too strong and so one's needs are not met.

How are conflicts resolved? George Mahl has pointed out that most everyday ones eventually are dealt with consciously; by thinking about what to do, by reasoning and finally deciding upon an alternative. (This process can be carried out with a series of steps listed in Chapter 11.) But some do not get resolved this way, either because the emotions connected with them are too strong, they are currently impossible to solve, or because a person will not admit a conflict exists. One clear example is a girl brought up in a very prim and proper household confronting a strong sexual attraction for someone, or a man feeling a homosexual attraction and hating himself for it.

What can then happen is that the conflict gets repressed, blotted from conscious awareness, as Sigmund Freud elegantly described. This repression was shown in some studies of experienced and inexperienced sport parachutists by Epstein and Fenz in the 1960s. Jumping out of a plane is a very stressful event and the physiological index of stress was about the same in amateurs and pros. But the pros seemed much more relaxed and calm because they had evidently repressed the conflict between jumping and staying on the plane. The amateurs had not. But, when they finally hit the ground, the anxiety came at full flood for the pros. One gets similar reactions after other stressful events, such as a traffic accident.

Mahl also pointed out that repressed unconscious conflicts can lead to maladaptation. First, they rarely get resolved and so much frustration can result from one's needs not being met. Second, one may pay a great psychic price to keep the conflict repressed. Third, they can lead to what Mahl calls otherwise inexplicable over-reactions. He gives an example of a man having a trying day at the office with many provocations that needed to be inhibited. When he gets home he may shout at his wife and children for very little reason.

FAULTY THINKING As mentioned in Chapter 1, stress occurs through a troubled transaction with the environment. A major function of the mind is to minimize that troubled transaction, to enable us to understand the world well enough to know what dangers to avoid and how to meet our basic needs. And, when the environment changes, it enables us to think through problems and work out more adaptive ways of behaving.

So, a major part of adjusting is tailoring one's thinking, one's ideas, to the world as it changes. Maladaptation can occur from a failure to do this, a clinging to old ways of thinking that are no longer appropriate or never were. One example of this was the conduct of the Vietnam War by US generals. David Halberstam in *Making of a Quagmire* suggests that the Americans thought in concrete terms, in terms of fixed structures like bridges, roads, and arms caches, as in World War II. The Vietcong were much more flexible, not thinking in terms of fixed structures, or even fixed fighting fronts. If one trail was destroyed, they just cut another one. They infiltrated and fought minor actions in many different places at once. American military planners never fully adapted their thinking to fight such an enemy. Indeed, it is an old military saying that generals are always trying to fight the previous war over again.

Some more mundane examples and ways to overcome faulty thinking are given in much greater detail in Chapter 10.

CHANGE

If one described the world with a single word, "changeable" would be a good choice. Our physical and social environments are in continual flux. Daylight changes to night, the seasons, drought, floods and earthquakes alter the landscape, people around us change, die, or move away, and others move in. Our bodies continually change as we get older. Our society itself is altering rapidly, in superficial ways like fashions in dress, music, and celebrities to more important ones like social roles and rules. Since as recently as 1970, for example, the role of women has altered dramatically, and all of us in some way have had to adjust to it. The nature of the family in the last decade has altered. No longer is the husband usually the sole breadwinner, with the wife staying home minding the house and children. Now both are likely to work, their roles being quite different than before, and both needing to split up the necessary household tasks. Change is an intrinsic part of life, to which we must continually accommodate ourselves. We are always arriving and departing, failing and succeeding, winning and losing, creating and destroying.

Change involves transitions, shifts from one stage of life, of thinking, of work, residence, country, and so on to another. According to Hopson (1981), many such major transitions occur in seven stages. The first stage he calls *immobilization*. This is when one realizes a transition is taking place and is simply overwhelmed by the adjustment. One cannot seem to think clearly, to plan, to learn the new skills required. Imagine a migrant to a new country confronted by new ways that seem incomprehensible. The second stage is *minimization*, where a person tries to trivialize, or

41

minimize the extent of disruption. Third is *depression*. This can occur when a person feels that some lifestyle changes are necessary, and has a sense of powerlessness about this. He or she may feel that events are out of control.

Fourth comes *letting go*. Here a person releases his or her tenuous hold on the past (for example, from a just departed lover, or city once lived in). The person tries to accept events for what they are and says "Here I am, now". Fifth is *testing*, where a person becomes more active, testing out new behaviors, new ways of coping with the new situation. Sixth is *search for meaning*, trying to understand the new stage or place of life, seeking meaning for the way things are now. And last is *internalization*, where a person becomes part of the new environment or situation. Here adjustment is complete.

This series will not fit every person, and certainly not every transition. It is best seen only as an interesting guide to what may happen to some people. The problem is, however, that wide individual differences occur in response to such transitions. Silver and Wortman (1980) argue that many people may never really get to that final halcyon stage, never let go and move on to the next phase of life. A parent, for example, may never really recover from a child's death.

Too great or too fast a rate of change can be very stressful, as Lauer and Lauer (1976) have noted. This belief is echoed in the traditional well-wishing of the Mexican peasant, "May you go with God and may nothing new happen to you". Too much can overtax one's powers to cope, leave one disoriented, with no firm bases upon which to grip. Many studies have shown that too many life changes in a short time (for example, shifts in job, residence, spouse and so on) can leave one more susceptible to physical diseases. For instance, people who have just had an interpersonal crisis are much more likely to get a streptococcal infection than other types of illness. According to some reports, many cancer victims have suffered a significant loss in the two years before getting the disease. A study by Holmes and Masuda (1973) found that a person going through many life changes is much more likely to get a whole variety of physical and emotional disorders.

Holmes and Rahe (1967) put together a scale to measure the amount of recent life change (and presumably the stress) one is currently undergoing. Their scale is shown in Table 1, and is called the Social Readjustment Rating Scale.

Table 1
The Social Readjustment Rating Scale
(From Holmes and Rahe, 1967)

Mean Value	Life Event
100	Death of spouse
73	Divorce
65	Marital separation from mate
63	Detention in jail or other institution
63	Death of a close family member
53	Major personal injury or illness
50	Marriage
47	Being fired at work
45	Marital reconciliation with mate
45	Retirement from work
44	Major change in the health or behavior of a family member
40	Pregnancy
39	Sexual difficulties
39	Gaining a new family member *(e.g., through birth, adoption, oldster moving in, etc.)*
39	Major business readjustment *(e.g., merger, reorganization, bankruptcy, etc.)*
38	Major change in financial state *(e.g., a lot worse off or a lot better off than usual)*
37	Death of a close friend
36	Changing to a different line of work
35	Major change in the number of arguments with spouse *(e.g., either a lot more or a lot less than usual regarding child-rearing, personal habits, etc.)*
31	Taking out a mortgage or loan for a major purchase *(e.g., for a home, business, etc.)*
30	Foreclosure on a mortgage or loan
29	Major change in responsibilities at work *(e.g., promotion, demotion, lateral transfer)*
29	Son or daughter leaving home *(e.g., marriage, attending college, etc.)*
29	Trouble with in-laws **(Continued overleaf)**

Table 1 (Continued)

Mean Value	Life Event
28	Outstanding personal achievement
26	Wife beginning or ceasing work outside the home
26	Beginning or ceasing formal schooling
25	Major change in living conditions *(e.g., building a new home, remodelling, deterioration of home or neighborhood)*
24	Revision of personal habits *(dress, manners, association, etc.)*
23	Troubles with the boss
20	Major change in working hours or conditions
20	Change in residence
20	Changing to a new school
19	Major change in usual type and/or amount of recreation
19	Major change in church activities *(e.g., a lot more or a lot less than usual)*
18	Major change in social activities *(e.g., clubs, dancing, movies, visiting, etc.)*
17	Taking out a mortgage or loan for a lesser purchase *(e.g., for a car, TV, freezer, etc.)*
16	Major change in sleeping habits *(a lot more or a lot less sleep, or change in part of day when asleep)*
15	Major change in number of family get-togethers *(e.g., a lot more or a lot less than usual)*
15	Major change in eating habits *(a lot more or a lot less food intake, or very different meal hours or surroundings)*
13	Vacation
12	Christmas
11	Minor violations of the law *(e.g., traffic tickets, jaywalking, disturbing the peace, etc.)*

Each life event is given a certain score in life-change units. For example, divorce is given the high score of 73 units because it usually means a massive life change. Christmas gets the smaller score of 12. You get a total score for the last two years by adding up values for the events that have happened to you after multiplying them by the number of times they occurred. The higher your final score, the more change you are undergoing and theoretically the more susceptible you are to ailments.

Thomas Holmes suggests a number of ways to use the scale in order to reduce stress. A few of these are as follows. First, he suggests, become familiar with the life events and the scale value of change for each. Second, try to recognize when an event will occur and think about how you might best adjust to it. Third, try to anticipate life changes and plan for them a long time before they hit. And fourth, try to pace yourself, not hurrying too much at all.

But the scale should not be given undue weight. It is best seen as an interesting guide to the stress of life events and how much we may at present be suffering. The problem is, though, that such events will have different effects on different people. First, we all need different amounts of change. Some will only be happy with a lot, be they positive or negative, and so a high score for them may mean something different than a high score for a person who likes a stable, predictable life. Second, a certain life change for one person may mean a great reduction in stress. Divorce is one obvious example. A couple having numerous fights and living in a tense, frosty atmosphere may find their separation a very positive event, with a shift to a calmer state of mind for both.

Let us now look in detail at some of the major stress-inducing life changes and how people may adapt to them. Most are ones that we all must negotiate eventually.

LOSS   This is an unavoidable part of living; at times we gain and at others we lose. All of us must give up or have wrenched from us numerous important things over time, many as an intrinsic part of maturing. We lose the simple, carefree days of childhood, our early friends and lovers as they move away or change, our youth, and ultimately life itself. Other losses are not so inexorable and unpreventable but still strike many a person. They include loss of a job, of a house through a natural disaster or finance problems, loss of a loved one such as a spouse, loss of a limb or movement, or good health.

Of these, one which can hit very hard is loss of a spouse, either through death or divorce. Generally, the survivor has to adjust to life without an almost constant companion, to one without some important social roles, to indeed begin again. As a result, virtually every society sets aside a period of mourning for them. Widows and widowers are given time to work through their loss, to try to adapt to it. Such a period of pain and mourning appears to be necessary. In Western society, usually up to a year is allowed for recovery.

Mourners may go through a series of stages after a significant loss. Clayton (1968) describes the initial reaction as a "depressive complex". It consists of loss of appetite, loss of interest in just about everything, tiredness much of the time, and perhaps wishing to be dead. A study by Wiener, Gerber, Battin and Arkin (1975) looked at a group of people who had just lost a loved one. The initial feelings were quite consistent in all of them; sadness and depression, a feeling of emptiness without the deceased, discontent, loneliness, sad and happy memories of life with the person when he or she was still alive.

Common is a belief that the lost person will somehow come back, and the frequent mistaking of strangers for him or her. Also common is anger directed at the loved one for departing, at the self for imagined misdeeds against him or her, or at others. At some point survivors may start to look around for someone to blame, someone to punish. Hence we may get numerous lawsuits directed at drivers after a fatal accident, at doctors after a failed operation, and so on. An interesting study of some widows of policemen slain in the course of duty showed most to have very deep feelings of anger toward the community, seeing society as too soft on criminals.

Other workers such as Hinton (1967) have described a frequent reaction in the initial stages of loss as emotional numbness, which can last a few hours to several weeks. A person may seem to function well and show no obvious sign of sorrow for some time. Along with the feelings of despair or emptiness, a person may suffer waves of yearning for the lost one, and many psychosomatic symptoms. Restlessness, especially at night, is common. Guilt feelings may come a little later, guilt about surviving him or her. This acute phase may only last a couple of weeks, but can continue much diminished for up to a year. Eventually there may follow a period of resolution, the person coming together again, putting aside the shackles of the past and looking ahead. The survivor may accept life as it is and try to get on with the business of living.

But as mentioned above, many do not so recover. The loss may permanently alter their view of the world. For instance, a person before a child's death may have looked at the world as an orderly place where things go mostly to plan. After it, he or she may see it as a capricious place where senseless events occur. As well, many individuals do not go through clear, orderly stages when recovering from a loss.

Another interesting fact is that the above pattern may hold for other kinds of loss as well, such as of a job, a house, a limb, and so on. Persons deeply involved in a well-liked job may also greet the onset of unemployment with all the signs of having lost a loved one.

MIGRATION Ambrose Bierce in *The Devil's Dictionary* defined "immigrant" as "an unenlightened person who thinks one country better than another". But with humor aside, shifting from one abode to another is often a radical life change. Emigrants from one land to another must often leave much behind; relatives and friends, familiar places and ways of thinking, and their solid niche in society. All this they give up for an alien culture and society. Even a shift within the same nation can take much readjustment; from finding a new job to building up a new network of friends.

Migration has been very widespread this century. Waves of European immigrants seeking a better life swelled the populations of North and South America greatly. The last fifty years has seen an incredibly vast flow of refugees. World War II left Europe in chaos for years afterward, with literally millions of displaced persons whose homes and past lives had been destroyed. Many were later dispersed all over the world; to the United States, Australia and Israel, especially. More recently, the Soviet invasions of Hungary in 1956, Czechoslovakia in 1968 and Afghanistan in 1979 created a flood of political refugees, as did the Indo-China conflict.

Even within the industrialized countries, there has been a tidal-wave surge of the rural population moving into the cities.

And, many people frequently change their residence or city in search of a promotion or better living conditions.

The transition to a new home can be a shock, leaving the migrant for a time off-balance and disoriented. There may be much grieving for the lost home, especially if the shift was forced, as with refugees. This feeling of being uprooted, of losing links with all that was familiar, may cause symptoms like those of losing a loved one. People may respond initially by intensifying their family relations, others by somehow trying to stay mentally close to their old area. It is an interesting fact that the word "nostalgia" was first coined to describe such a mental state of homesickness, then "caught" by Swiss mercenaries serving in European armies. Doctors saw it as an actual disease, an illness like measles or mumps, caused by separation from home.

Indeed, some migrants never seem to adjust, and eventually have to return home. Others go home after making their fortunes. In some third world countries many young men leave their villages to work in the cities for a few years. In Malaysia a favorite profession is driving a pedicab. The life is hard, and they may sleep on these machines only for a few hours at night near bus and ferry terminals. But when they have made some money, it is back to the village to marry, buy some land and settle down.

The pressures of such a life change as migration can be seen from mental hospital admission rates for immigrants. They tend to be much higher than one would expect. Some researchers have proposed that this is because many migrants already have some existing emotional disturbance. Thus they never can seem to fit in anywhere and keep searching for something better, or things just get so bad at home that they need to go. It is more likely, though, that migration is such a stressful event for so many that they can collapse before reaching a stable adjustment. As well, the reception that immigrants get can make a great difference. Some groups face discrimination and herding into ghettos from which it may take generations to eventually leave. And of course, whether a migrant is willing to assimilate into the new culture is important.

The most dramatic need for adaptation is when moving to a radically different culture. Consider the rural Vietnamese used to Buddhist ways of thinking shifting to the competitive, hectic USA. One's ways of thinking, of doing basic things like selecting a mate, finding a job or place to live and one's interests may all be totally inappropriate. Weinberg pointed out that migrants can almost seem like newborn babies, knowing nothing about the new world, being helpless, and almost seeming to have to start from scratch. Clearly it helps if the migrant is well-briefed on what to expect before leaving and if he or she is given much time to reflect on the new experiences and how to adapt to them. Thus the host country should not put great early pressure on immigrants to conform and assimilate. Adjusting to a new environment can take years. A study by Brody (1976) of two hundred Hungarian families settling in the USA after the 1956 uprising found that it took between one and three years for most of them to feel at home.

An interesting study by Saul Levine (1976) illustrates some possible stages in adjustment to a new country. He interviewed a small number of the estimated one-hundred thousand young Americans who fled to Canada during the Vietnam War to avoid the draft. As well as the radical shift, they had to often face the twin stresses of poverty and lack of family support for their actions. He found that, not too surprisingly, the dodgers were better adapted after the shift if they had lived away from home before. Evidently, this would have given them more idea of what to expect, among other things. Also, they were better adapted if their expectations about Canada were not unduly unrealistic; that is, they had not seen it as paradise, freedom, the road to nirvana and so on.

The initial stage after arrival seemed to be *disorganization*. They found themselves confused and floundering in the somewhat different culture. Isolation, loneliness and perhaps some guilt about leaving was there for some. The second stage, which not all went through, was *acting out*, that is, giving expression to latent, often hostile, impulses normally kept suppressed. Those that did may have begun fairly destructive relationships with others, or engaged in criminal activity, and some may impulsively have decided to return to the USA. The third stage was *searching*, where the person pricked up his ears, opened his eyes and looked at himself, his relationships, and for some meaning in life. They more realistically appraised their lives. The fourth and final stage Levine called *adaptation* and *integration*, where the person started to identify himself as a

Canadian, concerned with Canadian issues, problems and politics. Evidently he developed close personal ties and a sense of belonging. Not many had made it that far at the time of Levine's study, however.

SOCIETAL AND SOCIAL-CLASS CHANGE As mentioned earlier, this century has seen some of the most radical changes in society yet seen. In much of the world, the secure village where everyone knows everyone is being eroded away. In the East, materialism and urbanization are eroding traditional Buddhist and Hindu values. Many traditional South Sea Island cultures have been shattered by the introduction of new ideas, one notable example being the notion of money. Our own society is also altering rapidly, partly through massive advances in technology and better communications. All this kind of ferment can be very difficult for older people, used to more settled ways and values, to handle. In some ways they may experience the social change like a migrant from one culture greeting another.

A similar shift is between social classes, a quite common event these days. A particular social class can seem like a mini-culture, with its own attitudes, behavior patterns, mores and rules. Middle-class people in Western society, for example, tend to value education, working to own a house, and are oriented toward the future. Upper-class people often have different rules; never to act too concerned about anything, for example, and to greatly value certain leisure activities. The classes also may raise their children quite differently. As a result, an upwardly mobile working-class person entering the middle class through education (or whatever) may find the event quite a stressor. He or she may be confronted with a new set of rules and attitudes to acquire.

TIMES OF STRESS IN THE LIFE CYCLE

Much of the stress of life occurs at particular points, at ages which mark the transition from one stage of life to another. Sailing is often smooth until such a point. As we mature, our development is marked by such times of crisis, during which we need to shift to new roles, new ways of dealing with others, new modes of living. The most dramatic such transition is birth — an abrupt radical passage from relative peace and tranquillity to our changeable, uncertain world. (Ambrose Bierce defined "birth" as "the first and direst of all disasters".) From thereabouts onward we face a series of quite predictable development points; starting school, adolescence, leaving home, beginning work or university, marriage, the age-thirty crisis, the midlife crisis, the empty nest, through to retirement and old age. Much has been written about this well-trod path along which we all journey and the special problems posed at each point. One best-selling popularization is Gail Sheehy's 1976 book *Passages: Predictable Crises of Adult Life*.

Some earlier and more academic efforts to chart this course go back a long way. One carried out by Havighurst (1972) describes the tasks, the problems that we need to solve at various phases of life; for example, early adulthood, middle age and "later maturity". These range from taking a spouse and finding a peer group in early adulthood (up till age thirty) to adapting to retirement and declining physical powers in one's twilight years. A more recent description comes from the work of Levinson and his colleagues, a chart of which appears in Table 2.

Let us now look in more detail at some major transitions.

ADOLESCENCE For many, adolescence is a time of storm and stress, evidently being so across most or all cultures. It marks the change from childhood to adulthood, with its many new roles, responsibilities and expectations to live up to. It marks the real start of sexuality, and the search for intimacy with others. It requires adjustment to one's physical changes, gaining a new body image and adapting to others' new reactions to it. People become much less dependent on their family, before this point the major source of emotional support. The peer group becomes very important, adolescents usually being very conformist and concerned with what others in their age group think of them. Indeed, in Western society, adolescents often form a subculture which seems incomprehensible to their elders. Finally, it is the time when most must decide on a career, a vocation.

Erik Erikson characterizes this time as a period of searching for identity. A person asks, "Who am I and what will I become?" Later adolescence is also often the occasion of leaving the family home; either by going out to work or moving to study at a college or university.

51

Table 2
Periods of Development of Men during Early and Middle Adulthood

Periods of Development	Ages
Leaving the Family Transition • *effort to establish oneself independent of the family.*	16—18 to 20—24
Getting into the Adult World • *a new home base* • *exploration and commitment to adult roles* • *fashioning an initial life structure*	early 20s to 28
Age Thirty Transition • *reassessment of life structure*	28 to 30
Settling Down • *establishing a stable niche* • *making it: upward strivings* • *becoming one's own man: giving up mentors, emphasizing parts of the self and repressing others*	early 30s to 38
The Mid-Life Transition • *reassessment of life structure*	38 to early 40s
Restabilization to Middle Adulthood	middle 40s

(From Levinson, Darrow, Klein, Levinson, and Braxton, 1974.)

Not surprisingly, this stormy period often presents seemingly insurmountable hurdles for many. Indeed, adolescence frequently marks the beginning of many of the classic emotional disorders, schizophrenia being one notable example. Perhaps these arise partly because a person cannot satisfactorily adjust to the necessary changes.

MARRIAGE AND CHILDREN Most people are married by their late twenties. Until recently, staying single was not much of a realistic option, especially for women. The social pressure to wed was quite horrendous. Marriage takes much adjustment. Both partners must learn new roles; being a husband or wife and later a father or mother. Rausch, Goodrich and Campbell (1976) note some major adjustments new couples must make; working out acceptable sexual relations, handling money, maintaining a household, working out effective ways to communicate with each other, relating to each other's families and friends, aligning to each other's habits, and making plans for future education and careers. This is just part of a long list. And the nature of the marriage itself changes over time. The beginning and end points were humorously described by Voltaire as follows, "It begins with a prince kissing an angel and ends up with a bald-headed man looking across the table at a fat woman."

While marriage can seem like a major life upheaval many new parents say that it was nothing compared to the arrival of their first child. Many remark that they just did not realize what a dramatic change a baby would make. Marital satisfaction often plummets for a time here. A study by Dyer (1976) of new parents showed much consistency in their reactions. Most complained of exhaustion, not getting enough sleep through giving constant attention to the newcomer. They needed to get used to being up at all hours, getting by on one income if the wife had been working beforehand, and adjusting to new routines. Both spouses reported finding it hard to adapt to being tied down so much more at home, and many wives reported feelings of neglecting their husbands in favor of the child. Another common complaint is of becoming distanced from still-childless friends. Le Marr says that the couple is "jolted from the honeymoon stage".

THE AGE-THIRTY TRANSITION Many go through another adjustive crisis some time between the ages of twenty-eight and thirty-two. Age thirty by many estimates marks the passage from youth to maturity, with a new set of expectations from others. Gail Sheehy calls it "catch 30". One is expected to settle down, to a homelife or a career. The frivolity of youth is gone. It can be a time of reassessment of life goals, of career plans, of the meaning of life and what one will do with the rest of it. Divorce is apparently most likely around this time if it is to occur: when the man is around thirty and the woman twenty-eight.

THE MIDLIFE CRISIS This can occur any time from the middle thirties up to the early forties. Age forty might be the median point. Here, a person may shift to a radically different lifestyle, partly because of a sense that time is running out, of ageing. Depression is the most common symptom. Levinson et al. (1974) described it as follows:

The mid-life transition occurs whether the individual succeeds or fails in his search for affirmation by society. At 38 he thinks that if he gains the deserved success, he'll be all set. The answer is, he will not ... the central issue is not whether he succeeds or fails in achieving his goals. The issue, rather, is what to do with the experience of disparity between what he has gained in an inner sense from living within a particular structure and what he wants for himself ... To put it differently it is not a matter of how many rewards one has obtained; it is a matter of the goodness of fit between the life structure and the self.

Levinson says that many of us have a dream as young adults, a dream about what we will be, what we can achieve. A severe crisis can hit later when a person suddenly realizes that his present life is very different from that of the dream, or that he or she has betrayed or compromised it.

A study by Gould (1972) sheds more light on these and later years. He interviewed 524 middle-class men and women between sixteen and sixty years old. Some of the more interesting findings were that people began to have a sense that time was running low by their mid-thirties, that they may not be able to accomplish all they set out to, and becoming more ready to accept what they really can do with their lives. They were also more likely to become dissatisfied with their marriages, and to take more interest in their children. By the early forties, people are more unstable, feel more uncomfortable but this syndrome tapers off over the next few years. Finally, halcyon days may come later, with happy marriages, and much interest in friends and children.

RETIREMENT AND OLD AGE At this stage, from around sixty-five years on, people begin to regret losing the physical beauty of youth and worry about their physical decline and the chances of a variety of diseases associated with old age. They may focus on putting together all their life experiences, and coming to terms with the inevitability of death. It also may be a time of withdrawal from many active social contacts, of looking more inwardly at the self. Erik Erikson said that the major task to complete in this phase is to develop a sense of wholeness and adequacy as a human being, without the daily responsibilities of job and family.

CHAPTER 4

Coping and Adapting to Extreme Stressors

In the middle of the 1978 academy-award-winning film *The Deerhunter* is a very powerful scene. The setting is the Vietnam War and the three heroes and some other US soldiers have been captured by the Vietcong. They are held in a camp on a river in which their gaolers keep themselves amused by forcing their charges to play Russian roulette, and betting on who will "win". Two prisoners have to sit opposite one another, alternately pulling the trigger of a pistol containing a single bullet. The "game" goes on until one player is unlucky enough to strike the loaded chamber and blows his head off. A prisoner who will not play goes into a bamboo cage half-submerged in the river, to soon die. So the choice is between certain death in the cage, albeit a slow one, or a fifty per cent chance of a rapid demise if one can muster the strength to pull the trigger.

With death staring each soldier in the face, the situation is one of horrendous stress, and the different ways the Americans react is very well depicted. One, already some time in the cage, has clearly given up, and with no hope passively awaits death. This extreme apathy response is called the Musselman syndrome, and we look at it in more detail soon. Two others are taxed beyond their coping powers, the stress overwhelming both. Each stammers, and cannot act effectively. Yet one GI, played by Robert de Niro, still has the strength and presence of mind to try to find a way out. He convinces the captors to let him play the game with three bullets instead of one, tempts fate by going through three empty chambers, and finally helps dispatch the guards with the pistol.

This scene illustrates well an extreme situation, one in

which the people caught up are pushed to the limits, and beyond, of their ability to cope. There are many such situations, some of which we have already mentioned. They range from combat, torture, exposure to enemy bombing, hurricanes, fires, floods and long-term imprisonment to one of the worst of all, the Nazi concentration camp. They are extremely stressful either because injury, life itself, or all one's property is threatened or one's hold on a stable, predictable world is shattered. With some such as concentration camps or prisons a person's self-esteem and feelings of worth as a human being may be constantly under attack.

Studying such extreme situations can tell us much about stress and coping. Examining reactions to war, for example, has taught us a great deal. Psychiatrist Peter Bourne makes an interesting analogy between advances in physical medicine during war and advances in the understanding of stress. He points out that surgeons learn a lot about surgery during wars because the flood of battlefield casualties both gives them practice and induces them to develop new techniques. So, when the surgeon goes back to private practice, his civilian patients gain much. Bourne suggests that our knowledge of stress has advanced in the same way.

The sections that follow examine a few extreme situations; the ways that people try to cope, and the long-term effects the experience may have. We look at two major types of extreme situations; the short kind over relatively quickly, and the longer kind, which can last years. Some similarities in human reactions to extreme stress become apparent, and the ways in which some coping methods examined in Chapter 2 are used will become clear.

COMBAT

Wartime is very stressful for soldiers for a number of different reasons. First is the most obvious: the ever-present danger of unexpected death; from an enemy bullet, shell, bayonet or another of the many lethal devices that nations are so adept at creating. (Yossarian in Joseph Heller's *Catch 22* had an unusual reaction to this threat when he exclaimed with great surprise that people were trying to kill him. That the enemy was trying to kill everyone on his side was irrelevant to him.) This fear of death can persist for months at a time. Wars often involve protracted battles. An example is the siege of the US Marine base at Khe Sanh during the Vietnam War. It lasted seventy-seven days, during which time the enemy lobbed up to 1500 shells a day into the camp, and B-52s continually bombed the perimeter. A particularly nightmarish image of such a situation is a scene from the 1977 film *Apocalypse Now*, also set in Vietnam. A base has the sole purpose of keeping a bridge up and open. GIs build it up by day and the enemy knocks it down again after sunset. At night, shells explode everywhere, GIs fire at virtually anything that moves. No one seems to be in command of the camp. Terrified soldiers pack their bags and try to flee on any passing river transport.

Combat is stressful for other reasons. There can be great physical deprivation: bad food or none at all, little sleep, much noise, exposure to the elements, long periods in a state of anxious alertness and also much monotony. A British officer during the 1982 Falklands War repeated a venerable quote, "War is long periods of utter boredom punctuated with short periods of utter terror". As well, the sheer act of fighting requires a personality change. The soldier has to go from being a peaceful citizen, taught from childhood that killing another is a heinous crime, to a homicidal fighting machine. It is no wonder that some people just cannot adapt.

How, then, do untried soldiers handle the stress of combat? How, for example, during the Napoleonic wars could troops march in formation towards the enemy as cannonballs ripped right and left through their ranks. How is such composure achieved?

Both Moran (1966) and Kellett (1982) have summarized a number of methods. Some that these authors mention are as follows. In the very first exposure to war, many report having an unearthly feeling that they are invulnerable, or that they are more like a spectator, watching the fight from a distance, than a participant. Robert Crisp (1959), a World War II tank commander, described his feelings just before a battle in North Africa in 1941:

*Not for one moment did I contemplate the possibility of
anything unpleasant, and with that went an assumption that
there was bound to be a violent encounter with the enemy,
that it would end in our favour, and that if anything terrible
were going to happen it would probably happen to other
people but not to me.*

This feeling is denial, suppression of stressful thoughts.
P. G. Bourne reported the same defence mechanism in helicopter
ambulance crews in Vietnam. Their job was regarded as one of
the most dangerous of all. They had to swoop into the battlefield
under enemy fire, pluck the wounded from it, and fly out again.
Yet they typically denied that their job was particularly
dangerous. They also used a statistical defence, pointing out that
the chances of death on any particular mission were low. Janis
(1971) has argued that this protective denial eventually gets
shattered; by seeing what enemy weapons can do, by experiencing a near miss or by seeing a friend die. Other devices used to
cope are fatalism and superstition. Israeli army psychologist
Sohlberg described their use among his nation's soldiers in the
1973 Yom Kippur War. One might say "If I am going to die, that
is my fate. There is nothing to be done about it", or "What will be
will be". A soldier might also go through a series of rituals that
were supposed to ward off the chances of being wounded or killed.

Another powerful method soldiers use to deal with fear is
distraction. They keep their minds busy with the business of
fighting or with purely technical matters and so do not allow
themselves to think about the danger. Robert Crisp again:
"When mind and body are fully occupied, it is surprising how
unfrightened you can be".

Fright also can be much reduced by the presence of one's
buddies. Buddy groups are very important in wartime, many
soldiers reporting that they eventually fight not for country or
principle but for their mates.

Yelling is also used to lessen fear. The Japanese soldiers in
World War II would shout "banzai", Zulu warriors had their
war chants, and the Confederates in the US Civil War their
famous "rebel yell". Robert de Niro in *The Deerhunter* when
pulling the trigger of the gun against his head would yell loudly to
help him do it.

But such methods will not work forever. Too prolonged a spell of combat can lead to overwhelming stress and the "battle-fatigue" syndrome. The symptoms include anxiety and depression, agitation, general disorganization of thinking and behavior, and often apathy. In World War I, the syndrome was called shell shock. Troops appeared dazed, had hand tremors and would jump at just about any sudden sound.

Battle fatigue seems to be brought on by a sheer accumulation of stressors which the soldier does not have a chance to recover from. In World War II, psychiatrists estimated that a soldier was worn out after eighty to one hundred cumulative days of combat. Then he was just too cautious or hypertensive to everything around. The syndrome was also more likely to occur if soldiers were taken unexpectedly from safety to battle. Evidently time to prepare for fighting was very important. By the years of the Vietnam War the causes and cure were pretty well understood, and the number of psychiatric casualties was low. Part of the reason for the low rates was that battles were usually very short (one to one and a half hours) and troops could be later whisked to a safe, secure place to rest. Treatment for those who did succumb was hospital rest near the the combat zone immediately after the symptoms appeared. And throughout treatment it was made clear that they were expected to recover rapidly and head back to the battlefield. Usually they did.

While the number of psychiatric casualties in Vietnam was low, it is said that many American and Australian veterans suffered a particular post-traumatic disorder, unlike soldiers of previous wars. Many faced great readjustment problems upon returning home. Shatan (1978) describes some symptoms; guilt about surviving and about activity in Vietnam, feeling a scape-goat, outbursts of uncontrollable rage against indiscriminate targets, and a sense of alienation and emotional detachment from self and others. Nightmares are common, a frequent theme being helplessness in the face of enemy attack. Sufferers may be bothered by superficially inexplicable nervous attacks which can be activated by everyday events. One example is a returnee who, three years after the war, told a psychiatrist that his baby daughter's crying made him fearful and anxious. Eventually it was traced to an incident during the war where he told a medic not to go near a crying baby until the area was checked. But the medic ignored him and was blown up.

The symptoms have much to do with the nature of the war and the home reception that veterans received. Bourne (1978) points out that there were no fixed lines and the slippery enemy was rarely seen. So, there was much displaced aggression, soldiers having "crazy times" in which they fired at random. It was very hard to tell Asian friend from foe, and many soldiers developed a hatred of all Asians. There was much brutalization on both sides. There was little social support in each man's unit, something which had kept many World War II soldiers fighting. Each man was there only for a year and then abruptly went home. So personnel in each unit changed a lot and each man felt that his only task was to survive his year-long tour of duty.

As well, unlike other wars, veterans were not received as heroes when they returned home. They were blamed for losing the war or were treated as fools for going in the first place.

THE CONCENTRATION CAMPS

Among the greatest horrors of history were the Nazi concentration camps. The conditions in which millions of people lived (many for years) were overwhelmingly stressful.

There were a multitude of stressors. First was the ever-present chance of sudden death. Daily, inmates were selected out for the gas chambers, and brutal guards would often kill for the slightest provocation. Other stressors were the very poor diet, epidemic diseases which could easily sweep through the extremely crowded quarters, general ill-treatment, heavy forced labor and so on. Viktor Frankl has written graphically about his experiences in one, saying that the whole environment was designed to make the individual feel worthless. When Allied troops finally entered the camps in 1945, they were appalled by what they saw. Here is a description from Belsen:

Incredible savagery — a studied policy of neglect, starvation, torture and extermination . . . so shocking it overtaxes imagination to grasp the reality . . . 40,000 emaciated apathetic scarecrows . . . defecate and urinate where they sit or lie . . . some 8000 to 10,000 naked decomposing corpses lay all over the camp. [Quoted by Collins, 1945.]

How did people survive and adapt to such Dantean vistas? The common reaction upon arrival was terror and shock. Then apathy would set in, followed by mourning and depression. These responses helped protect the individual for a while, some emotional blunting no doubt being necessary to stop being overwhelmed. A later mechanism often resorted to was denial. People just did not let themselves see the corpses or think about the terrors of the place. A quote from a study of survivors by Dimsdale (1974):

We were not very clever, we did not want to believe that anything was going on. There were rumors going around but we preferred to believe the versions that said that the Jews are collected in camps where they are treated all right.

And another:

We talked together as friends about concrete things, not about feelings. I think all the feelings were blocked; if you felt too much, you felt bad. To feel was to feel unpleasant, better not to feel at all, don't think about it.

Others regressed to childhood, becoming docile like children. Some began to identify with the sadistic guards. Inmates apparently feared "trustee" prisoners given authority over them more than their SS keepers. At the extreme, many fell into the state of severe apathy already mentioned called the Musselman syndrome. A person in its grip would not react to anything going on around, did nothing at all, apparently just waiting to die. Most who reached the stage and were not somehow shaken out of it by their comrades were usually killed immediately by the SS.

Another very important coping means which kept many people alive was survival for some clearly conceived purpose. Dimsdale's interviewees revealed the power of this basic motive. It might have been simply to see one's spouse or parents again, to seek revenge against the captors, or to bear witness to the world about what had happened. A survivor interviewed by Dimsdale put it this way:

I wanted to find my child, I wanted to be back with my husband. The feeling that somebody needs you is more important for survival than just the feeling that you have to survive. There were times that I did not feel like waiting for my food, thinking that I could get it tomorrow, but then I remembered my sister needed me and my husband needed me.

And another:

Once I saw a woman beaten with a whip by an SS man because she stole a carrot in the field where she worked. To see that young girl stretched out naked on the ground with the SS man beating her, I vowed I would never forget it.

A more intriguing method was to make oneself an object of study, a case study in coping with an impossible situation. And some evidently considered themselves already practically dead and lost any sense of danger. Another survivor interviewed by Dimsdale:

On the first day I learned that the SS would kill me eventually. I knew that I would die, that there was no possibility a man could go from the camps. The uncertainty was removed and also the fear; I became active in the camp underground. Each day we had many tasks — to save this person, watch the new transports, etc. We were so active in the camp underground that we did not pay any attention to the danger. I worked as a carpenter in the camps and always kept a cyanide pill if the SS should suspect me, catch me, and interrogate me.

Unfortunately, the long-term effects of their experiences upon the survivors were often dire. In the late 1950s many reports of the concentration-camp syndrome began to appear. The symptoms were anxiety, restlessness, apprehension, a strong tendency to be startled by ordinary but unexpected sounds, insomnia and nightmares. Many apparently had the feeling that their life was permanently arrested at the time of their camp experiences. They stayed forever at their age of internment. Many felt guilty at surviving when so many perished. Dimsdale described how some continually felt depression, despair, and a feeling of emptiness. They could find no order, no meaning in a universe in which such things could happen. Their personalities were often changed, people acquiring a permanent tendency towards apathy, dependence, and fatalism. Others were cursed with ingrained suspiciousness, cynicism and hostility.

63

DISASTERS

The forces of nature make our world a sometimes wild and unpredictable one. Every year tornadoes, floods, droughts, hurricanes, earthquakes, volcanoes and fires wreak a fearful toll on human life and property. The impact of such forces is often devastating. For example, in 1974 a tornado hit Zenia, Ohio, laying waste much of the town and killing a large number of residents. The wind was so powerful that papers were swept from filing cabinets and deposited 320 kilometres (200 miles) away.

How do people react to such sudden disaster? Often with great resilience as Janis (1976) describes. Many are at first in shock, and perhaps dazed and apathetic. This state can last for a few hours, then a person starts to function again. Panic is not common, and only tends to occur if escape routes are limited but not blocked completely. Survivor guilt, as among concentration-camp inmates, is also common. Later a person is likely to accept his lot as part of life, and adjust to the new circumstances. People also tend to band together much more closely in a crisis, and develop a strong support group.

A well-studied recent disaster occurred at the Hyatt Regency Hotel in Kansas City in 1981. On the evening of 17 July, two skywalk bridges collapsed on an estimated crowd of 2000 people. The final toll was 114 dead and over 200 injured.

Wilkinson (1983) interviewed 102 survivors of the tragedy, with some interesting findings. Almost ninety per cent reported a repeated reliving of the event, which for a significant number was serious enough to affect their daily lives. Other common symptoms were depression, anger at the hotel builders and management, sleep disturbances, and a ready startle response to many stimuli. Quite a few of the interviewees consciously avoided overhead bridges and balconies thereafter. Another symptom, reported by twelve persons, was survivor guilt. Several also said that they viewed life quite differently after the disaster. Typical comments were, "Now cannot overlook any suffering", "A strong desire for personal growth", "Enjoy life — it's fleeting", and "Feel closer to spouse, family, and friends".

The study also revealed a variety of coping methods used by the survivors in the aftermath. Many reported talking incessantly about the event, with virtually anyone who would listen.

Evidently they were trying to work through its meaning. Others said that they coped by trying to get back into the routine of work. Some merely took a holiday.

An interesting response to catastrophes was described by Janis (1971): staring. Many nearby residents may go to the site of destruction and literally spend hours motionless, looking at the devastation. Interviews with them suggest that they are trying to work through the meaning of the event, its meaning in terms of their own lives. For instance, a burst gas main once blew up a large house in Connecticut, killing all inside. Many locals stared fixedly all day at the gaping hole where the house had once been. As one such spectator put it:

I just stand here all day long looking across the street. I don't know why. I can't get over it. To think that they could be so alive the night before, playing cards, talking to us. Then all of a sudden, for no reason, they are wiped out. A big house is there one minute and the next minute nothing is left of it at all. I just can't understand it.

A similar response was often evident after a disaster of another sort, the killing of President Kennedy in 1963.

Another interesting phenomenon is a great fear, in the early stages of recovery, of a recurrence of the disaster. Victims of the Zenia tornado feared greatly another one, and reacted strongly to any wind above average force. Similarly, survivors of Hiroshima and Nagasaki dreaded additional US attacks. Rumors about another impending one were rife for days afterward. T. Hagashi, a doctor present during this crisis, said that the mere sight of a plane afterward would send people rushing into their shelters. Once again, the impact of the disaster reached far into the future for the A-bomb survivors, with fear reactions and so on persisting.

BATTERED WIVES

While this is very common, the situation can be as extreme as any of those covered above. Many women live in constant tension, fear and pain, subject to the capricious whims of a violent husband, often for many years. The dimensions of this problem are indeed great. Estimates are that half of American marriages are touched at some stage by domestic violence and many women cite it as their major reason for divorce. It occurs in all social classes. For a significant percentage of wives, violence is a chronic event to which the police and friends and relatives are indifferent. Victims can acquire the by now familiar stress symptoms of depression, anxiety, suspiciousness and various physical ailments. Social workers say that those who eventually do flee their circumstances can look like natural-disaster victims, appearing listless, depressed and years older than they really are.

Lenore Walker (1979) has suggested that violence in many homes runs in a fixed cycle. The first phase of it is one of slowly rising tension, which can last days or even years. Some minor beating may occur, and some relatively mild outbursts of anger. Tension builds and builds until the second phase arrives, marked by an eruption of full-fledged violence. Here a women may be very badly beaten, sometimes ending up in hospital. This phase can last anywhere between two hours up to a terror-filled week. After this explosion, the tension is resolved and a period of calm sets in. Here the husband may feel very guilty, and shower his wife with gifts, flowers and attention. He knows he has done wrong and wants forgiveness. But these halcyon days may not last long, and the tension-rising period begins anew.

Why do women stay in such an existence? There can be many reasons, given by Walker (1979). One is simply financial pressure. A wife may have no money of her own and no place to go. Alternatively, material circumstances may be very comfortable and so she decides that she will put up with the present threat to keep her fine home and place in society. Often the wife believes very strongly in the sanctity of marriage, that it should not be broken. Or, she may fear the husband's retaliation if she leaves. This fear is of course not groundless: women's refuges usually take great pains to keep their location secret. And some wives appear to feel that another relationship will be no different, that this is the way that men are and what most other marriages are like. They may come down with the learned-helplessness syndrome, losing faith in their self-efficacy. Certainly the circumstances are set to induce it. Thus, they may find it very hard to take any positive steps to get out of the situation. And finally, the wife may actually blame herself for any erupting violence, feeling responsible for provoking it. This is a form of denial. For example:

I'm not really sure how the whole incident happened. Perhaps it was my fault. Mike says he really didn't throw me against the stove. He just pushed at me and I fell and hit the stove. I really believe him. He couldn't have wanted to hurt me as badly as I was hurt. It really must have been an accident. [From Walker, 1979].

So, given that a wife is resigned to stay, how does she cope with the recurring anxiety? By some now familiar methods. One is withdrawal; into bed or into fantasy. Denial again is widespread. A wife may simply say there is no problem, or that the husband will change. Davidson (1978) also suggests that displacement of anger is common. Since directing anger toward the husband is usually quite dangerous, the wife may point it at others or herself. The children are a likely target. And, in some cases it may be the police trying to intervene in a domestic quarrel, who get turned upon by husband and wife alike.

Lenore Walker also suggests two other common coping methods; minimization and mastery. Minimization is like denial, a wife minimizes the seriousness of a particular event, or just selects out some benign feature of it. For example, one woman whose husband tried to choke her with a chain was grateful afterwards that it only made marks and not cuts. Or a violent attack might be shrugged off as a husband just having to let off a little steam every now and again. Mastery occurs during the tension-rising phase. Here a wife, with a good knowledge of what provokes and upsets her husband, organizes everything so that his lid will be kept firmly on. She may try to manipulate the behavior of other family members, or send her friends and relatives away for fear of causing an explosion.

PRISONERS OF WAR

In just about every war, soldiers from both sides are captured and imprisoned, sometimes for years. The conditions of captivity can be quite dire. Americans captured in Asian wars from World War II and Korea through to Vietnam had to live through particularly harsh circumstances. Over half of those prisoners held by the Japanese in World War II reportedly died in the camps. Forced marches and labor, poor diet, exposure to tropical diseases, isolation (sometimes for years) and attempts at "re-education" or "brainwashing" made the ordeal very stressful. Many died from a similar symptom of concentration camp inmates: a failure of hope to eventually get out.

Spaulding and Ford (1976) reported that two major types of personality were best equipped to survive such situations. One type was pretty shallow emotionally (and perhaps did not feel as much stress as a more sensitive person would) and also very manipulative in securing material goods. The other type was very mature mentally, and mobilized a whole series of coping techniques to survive. Some other personal qualities that helped cope with the Japanese camps were listed by Nardini (1962). Quick thinking and general cunning were very useful as was the ability to use fantasy and the power simply not to think about the closeness of possible death. People who were too dependent on others and too emotionally sensitive had much poorer survival chances. And, self-pity was highly dangerous to life.

A well-studied prisoner-of-war situation was the Pueblo incident of 1968. An American spy ship was captured in international waters by the North Koreans and the crew held for eleven months, while negotiations for their release went on. Spaulding and Ford (1976) examined the crew upon their return to the USA. The men had used a variety of different coping methods in captivity. Some used their faith in their commanding officer, their country and religion as a bulwark against thought reform by the captors. Some stayed emotionally detached from the situation, also rationalizing that eventually they would be let go. Group support against giving up was very important, the Pueblo group apparently being very tight-knit. Fantasy was used to while away the long monotonous hours; one reported that he rethought the electrical wiring of computers over the months. Upon their release there was a great similarity in their reactions. For a few days at least, the crew appeared subdued, mildly depressed and anxious. This reaction is somewhat similar to ex-prisoners of the Japanese, who tended to be seclusive and taciturn at release. This blandness gave way to anger and hostility, directed against the captors and perhaps other prisoners. Some psychiatrists believe that this reflects bottled-up guilt and anger which could not be expressed in captivity and which must be worked though. As a result, ex-prisoners of war in Vietnam were sometimes taken home by a slow hospital ship rather than by jet. Their adjustment problems could then be worked through in the care of specialists.

Prisoners of war are sometimes put in solitary confinement, either as punishment or because their ideas are dangerous from their captors' viewpoint. This social isolation is very stressful, because we are such a social species (see Chapter 5). Being alone too long can lead to delusions, anxiety, feelings of unreality. How do people cope with it? A study of captured American airmen in Vietnam was carried out by Hunter (1976). Their time in solitary had varied from about a month to five years. They appeared older than they actually were, and, not surprisingly, a bit abnormal according to psychiatrists' ratings. Those who handled the situation best again were those able to relax and put their imaginations to work providing entertainment. As one commentator put it:

Beyond their bodies, they kept their minds occupied by similar mental gymnastics. They built houses, roads, and bridges; they drilled oil wells; they dreamed and fantasized; they thought of families and classmates and friends; they did physics and math problems to several decimal places in their heads; they calculated money saved; and they looked inward at self.
[Quoted by Hunter, 1976.]

PRISONS

Most prisons are inhumane places. The stressors are numerous and long-lasting; no privacy, much noise, loneliness, overcrowding, being cut-off from all that is familiar, total dependence on the system, and battering to one's self-esteem from institutionalized abuse. There is the sheer sensory deprivation, the lack of interesting and varying stimulation that the outside world provides. As one prisoner put it, "It's like being in a submarine".

And there is the all-pervasive fear of violence from other prisoners, which Bill Sands in *My Shadow Ran Fast*, described as follows:

*Fighting makes a man lose his time off for good behavior ...
So there are no curses or insults — such as would lead to
fistfights on the outside. There are no fistfights. If the issue is
worth beefing about, it is done silently and quickly with a knife
or a length of pipe. There is a small scuffle, a man lies
bleeding; there is the clatter of a shive or pipe being kicked
away. If the weapon is ever found, it is not "on" anyone. There
are no fingerprints. That is all.*

*Everywhere, every minute — like the air you breathe —
there is the threat of violence lurking beneath the surface.
Unlike the air, it is heavy, massive, as oppressive as molasses. It
permeates every second of everyone's existence — the potential
threat of sudden, ferocious annihilation.* *

The Russian novelist Fedor Dostoevsky wrote about his years in prison in Siberia in *The House of the Dead*. After describing the bathhouse as filthy, stinking, steamfilled and crowded with naked bodies, he said that if he died and found himself in hell, it could be no worse. Yet people adapted to such conditions and Dostoevsky from his experiences described man as "a creature that can become accustomed to anything". This view was echoed by Wilfried Rasch in 1981 after a study of lifers in a German prison, "The results suggest the existence of a seemingly infinite human capacity to cope with the stress of an inhumane condition — long-term imprisonment ..."

Many of the coping methods prisoners use are those covered already. Withdrawal and emotional blunting, for example, are common. Here we look at some that arise particularly in prisons.

Lockwood (1982) describes some ways prisoners cope with the sexual harassment common in prisons. These include becoming violent to scare harassers off, joining a strong clique for protection, and staying in one's cell all the time.

In his book *The Felon*, John Irwin describes three major coping styles used by prisoners. The first is "doing time". Here a

---

* From Sands, B. *My Shadow Ran Fast*. Copyright 1964 by Prentice–Hall Inc. Published by Prentice–Hall, Inc. Englewood Cliffs, NJ 07632.

prisoner remains committed to his life in the outside world. He forms few friendships, and aims to get out as soon as possible through good behavior or other means. His focus is on the outside. The second is "gaoling". Here a prisoner cuts himself off from the outside and tries to make some kind of life in prison, to fully adapt to it, to come to terms with his situation. He may take the "inmate code" to heart as a result. Prisoners form their own social order in gaol with its special rules and mores. The code, according to Cohen and Taylor (1972), emphasizes loyalty, not losing one's head, not exploiting fellow inmates, not showing any weakness, asserting toughness and dignity, not being a "sucker" and not giving any prestige to the guards. The third style is "gleaning". Here an inmate tries to improve himself, reading educational books, taking university courses, learning more about himself and the world. Cohen and Taylor liken this "mind-building" to the extensive body-building popular in prisons.

Another way to cope is to acquire a new ideology, a new way of looking at the world. Prisoners may become religious, or take up Marxism. The latter was especially common among black prisoners in the USA. They came to see themselves not as criminals but as victims of capitalist and racist oppression. They organized behind bars. From the United Prisoners' Union in California in the early 1970s:

We as members of the convicted working class are twisted and mangled in the vice of a cruel system that cares little for human life. We are the last to be hired, the first to be fired. We are compelled to dance at every turn; we dance for a parole, and we dance for a job while on parole. In this widening class struggle in Amerika, we prisoners are the lowest of the low; we are wage slaves inside and outside ... [Quoted by Browning, 1972.]

Steven Roberts, writing in the *New York Times* in 1971, said that one lawyer called prisons a university for political education. Sacred books of black revolution such as Eldridge Cleaver's *Soul on Ice* and George Jackson's *Soledad Brother* were treasured.

Many prisoners also find ways to fight back at the system to try to keep their self-esteem. (Edward Coons said that prisoners have two basic complaints about prison: the monotony and the numerous ways you are made to feel you are finished as a man.)

The education method mentioned above is one way to hit back. A prisoner learns complex ideas and theories to bedazzle the guards and thus feel superior to them. Cohen and Taylor (1972) say that some prisoners become professional complainants, writing formal protests to politicians, prison authorities, humane organizations, and virtually anyone else who will listen. Others may take great pride in finding ways around regulations, of trying to outwit the oppressive order. Here is an amusing example of such behavior cited by Cohen and Taylor (1972), although from a non-prison situation, a man trying to avoid joining the army:

I eventually arrived at the last doctor, who asked me if I had ever suffered from various diseases . . . I said yes, I was in a bad motor accident — in hospital for a week and have suffered from bad headaches and dizzy spells ever since . . . Would you give information away to the Russians? I said . . . I would if given half the chance . . . why should I fight for this capitalist country? . . . After a while I . . . started to think of ways to show them I was mad . . . I leaped off the bed and started shadow boxing.

What kind of effects can long-term imprisonment have? There are scant data. But Rasch (1981) examined a sample of ninety-two lifers in a West Berlin gaol for signs of deterioration. To his surprise he found little. There was no evidence of an intellectual decline, although most of the inmates appeared depressed and emotionally withdrawn. In fact, almost half said their intellectual capacity had gone up during their term, evidently because of time to educate themselves. There was little sign of the psychoses and destruction of personality previous researchers had reported. In fact, upon their eventual release, their adjustment was rated good.

REACTIONS TO RAPE

This is the final extreme situation we look at. Its recorded incidence is quite high and many, many cases go unreported. The ordeal for the woman may not end with the actual event. As well as the harmful psychological effects of the experience, more trauma may result from hostile police or a defence attorney at the rapist's later trial.

Sutherland and Scherl (1976) carried out an interesting study of thirteen young American victims who had chosen to live in a slum area to work with poor people because of their idealistic beliefs. There were typical stages of reaction after the attack. Phase 1, which lasted up to a couple of days (though in some cases weeks), consisted of acute reaction. The signs included shock, disbelief and great dismay. Women often were very agitated, incoherent, and unable to discuss at all what had happened. In Phase 2, the victim usually returned to her normal everyday life; work, school, or home pursuits. She gave the impression of having adjusted to the event, but in most cases denial, rationalization and suppression of feelings were all that held her together. In Phase 3, she became depressed and needed to talk. Here at last the feelings brought on by the experience were somehow resolved and a real adjustment made.

But other studies suggest very great individual differences in reactions. These appear to depend much upon the victim's age, and the exact relationship between perpetrator and victim (Coleman, Butcher and Carson, 1980). For example, if the two are strangers, the woman is likely to have a strong fear of injury and death which can make the experience even more traumatic.

A study by Burgess and Holmstrom (1976) revealed two emotional styles among victims after the experience. The *expressed* style involved crying, sobbing and restlessness, showing the signs of inner fear. The *controlled* style involved an outward appearance of calm. Also common were by now familiar post-trauma symptoms: restlessness, insomnia, nausea and tension.

As with concentration-camp survivors, some victims may never fully recover. Burgess and Holmstrom (1978) found that over a quarter of the rape victims they studied did not feel they had recovered even four to six years later.

CHAPTER 5

Coping and the Social World

In nature, many species of animal fall pretty neatly into one of two categories; solitary or social. Members of a solitary species mostly live, hunt and die alone. Each may rarely see a fellow of the same breed and any accidentally encountered gets wide berth. Often individuals stick to little patches of territory, rarely straying outside their borders. Their once-in-a-season social contact may just be a mating partner.

In the other category are social species, such as ants, whales and various apes. Here, individuals live in groups of varying size and tightness. Chimpanzees, for example, live mainly in trees and their groups are very loose, allowing each chimp much freedom to do as he pleases. The baboon is closely related but lives on the far more dangerous ground, sharing it with various predators. Group organization here is far more strict, out of necessity, with much less individual freedom. They travel around the plain in a tight band, everyone in an assigned place. The young males go on the rim, where they can be sacrificed to a rampaging predator if necessary. The females and young go in the much safer interior. If each baboon conforms and acts out his role, the group will have better survival chances.

Humanity of course is also a social species. We live in groups ranging from the family, the basic unit of society, up to our nation or group of nations. Indeed, we belong to a great many groups throughout our lives, starting with the family and going on up to sets of playmates, teenage peer groups, workmates, and various professional associations and voluntary groups. These determine most of what we do, think, want, believe and indeed what we are; how we define ourselves. Our social environment is at least as important as our physical one. It is one to which we must adapt.

Adjusting to the social environment is critically important for two major reasons of concern here. The first is that the root source of stress for many people is difficulty in relating well to their fellows, adapting satisfactorily to their social circumstances. A person may not have the social skills, or the inclination to get on well with others, to make others like and accept them, and thus to create positive social climates. So, poor interactions with family, with workmates, and various others can be a continual source of severe stress. And it means that certain needs may not be met, needs that depend on good social skills, such as acquiring a partner or negotiating difficult disputes. And of course, as just about everyone eventually learns, one's advancement in life (especially in one's job) depends critically on how well a person gets on with superiors, also a task that requires developed social skills. The prospect of staying in the same dead-end, lower-rung job with bleak promotion prospects can be a constant stressor. Close relatives may help keep it so.

The second reason is that most of us quite desperately need the company, approval and support of other people. Maladjustment to the social environment may mean isolation and loneliness. Having too few contacts can be very stressful, as many isolated elderly people discover. Furthermore, a large number of studies have shown that being entrenched in a sound network of family, friends, and colleagues is itself a sound buffer against stress. Persons who lack the insulation that such a network provides seem to be much more susceptible to a range of stress-related ailments.

In this chapter we look at the concept of social networks in some detail, examining the different types that people may have, why they are so important in insulating against stress, and a few ways to build up one. Then we look at the notion of social skills in more detail, noting just what they are and some things that can go wrong in an unskilled person's handling of interactions.

SOCIAL NETWORKS

In the last decade or so a new branch of sociology impressively titled "network theory" has grown up and been applied to psychology and medicine. It is concerned with understanding the social networks that are so important to our health and well-being. Virtually everyone but the most isolated hermit has this kind of network.

A social network is much like those made up of television stations or telephones. There are nodes, which in a social network are people. Each node is connected to other nodes. Figure 2 gives a couple of examples.

Each circle is a node and represents one person. If there is

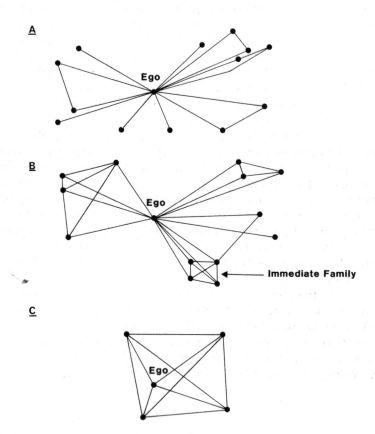

Figure 2 *Three different hypothetical networks. At the centre of each is ego, whose network each is. If two points are connected by a line, then the two people know and sometimes interact with each other.*

a line connecting two nodes, then the two people know each other, and interact at least sometimes. In 2A, from ego's point of view, he has a link to everyone and many have links to each other. But note that not all do. Thus ego knows some people who also know each other, but also some people who are strangers to each other.

Like most things, networks come in many shapes and sizes. They range from very closely to very loosely knit. In a closeknit one (as in 2C), everyone knows everyone else quite well. So all nodes are linked, and there are few or no connections outside the group. A religious sect, a stone-age tribe living in isolation or some families might look so. Many networks may be looser though, more like that in 2B. Here, there are far fewer connections. Thus, a person might know a string of people in one direction, say workmates, and another set such as old schoolmates or relatives who know few or none of the workmates. But there is some overlap. For example, a workmate might also be a close friend who knows one's relatives, old schoolmates, and members of one's bridge club.

Firstly, a few words about the connections themselves. They may be single or what sociologists call *multiplex*. This simply means that one either interacts with particular members of the network at one level, or at a variety of different ones. A single connection means that one has just one type of interaction with that person. With a workmate, one may talk about work-related matters only, and never see him outside working hours. Or one may have a friend who is a drinking companion or bridge partner and little else. With the more fancy multiplex ones, one has links at a variety of levels. So one might have a workmate who is a close confidant, also interested in one's favorite hobby, as well as someone to go to the racetrack with.

Secondly, the ties can be either supportive, neutral or negative, or a mixture of supportive and negative. A negative tie is one that gives little or no support but much flak. This could be a nagging spouse who does little else but provide abuse or a relative who continually borrows money and gives nothing in return. A positive tie could be a warm and supportive spouse or friend, or an understanding relative who is the proverbial shoulder to cry on. Neutral ties are just that: neither particularly positive nor negative.

Just how big are most people's networks and how many ties do they have of each kind? Studies have given us some idea. One described by Wellman (1981) was done in East York, a suburb of the large Canadian city Toronto. A total of 845 East Yorkers were asked about their ties to others, with some interesting results. Most reported having between sixteen and thirty-five significant others with whom they were in touch. Wellman says that this number tallies pretty well with other studies which have reported twenty to fifty such contacts. These, of course, are just their significant ones. Sociologists have estimated an average contact of some type with about one thousand to fifteen hundred others.

Interestingly enough, most East Yorkers said that the majority of their ties were not supportive. On the average only thirty per cent of their sixteen to thirty-five others could be relied on in an emergency, and only twenty-two per cent on everyday matters. Most also said that many ties were negative, only some positive and some mixed. The East Yorkers also reported that their ties were important in getting to enter new situations and new networks. Finally, a number of the respondents had several totally distinct networks. In other words, they had a network of one group of people radiating out in one direction plus a totally different one in another direction, with no connections between the two except that individual.

A person's network is important for a variety of reasons. First and foremost, most of us need others to give our lives any meaning. Few of us would be happy for very long without the stimulation of and sheer human contact with others. As mentioned, the network can be an integral part of our defences against stress. A sound network with at least some ties (or even just one close confidant) appears to buffer, insulate against stress. Numerous studies have shown this. One by Berkman and Syme (1979) compared people with low and high social contact; in other words people with few or no daily interactions with those who had many. Astonishingly, the low-contact group had a mortality rate two to four and a half times that of the high-contact group, over a long period. A variety of studies have also shown that people recover more rapidly from physical illness, such as a heart attack, when they have a good deal of emotional support (Gottlieb, 1981). A study by Eaton (1978) also showed that the stress of life events, like those examined in Chapter 3, had a much greater effect on persons unmarried or living alone, almost by definition people with lower total social contact.

Another suggestive example of this value of a network was a study carried out in Roseto, a community of Italian descent in Pennsylvania in the USA. In the early 1960s, the locals had very strong social networks, with close family ties and little competitiveness. They had a very low rate of a common sign of a stressful lifestyle — heart disease. But over time, their ties got weaker, and their society came to be like the more competitive, more alienated wider American society. By 1975, when the community had become Americanized, the death rate from heart disease had climbed to about the same level as the rest of America.

Networks reduce stress levels for several reasons. First, strong contacts can be counted on for material support when necessary. If money is needed to fix a car, to keep the landlord at bay another month, or even to buy some food, an isolated person probably will have more trouble getting it and is likely to suffer more. As well, contacts in a network are a useful source of advice, help, experience and new ideas about how to deal with one's stress-inducing problems. In Harlem this kind of important role is often filled by social-club owners. They are truly magnificent sources of advice and information because their job means they are the intersecting point of many networks. They have a good idea of what is available and what is going on, from where to get accommodation, to where jobs are coming, up to who might want to buy one's car. The same role to a lesser extent can be taken by bartenders and hairdressers, who hear a large number of people's troubles and often offer advice as well. Indeed, some community programmes aimed at improving the networks in a given area have put the local hairdressers and bartenders through training courses in counselling techniques.

Finally, networks are important because they can fulfil a basic human need when undergoing stress due to a crisis: the need to share reactions and thoughts with others. Best of all for this purpose is a group of people going through the same experience. They can be a source of advice on particular ways of coping with the crisis as well as people to swap feelings with. They can help a person better understand the life events that he or she is caught up in. Again, studies have shown the great benefit of belonging to such specially formed support groups. For example, one interviewed mothers going through the daily stress of just having had a premature baby. Many described their relief at just not having to face the experience alone as profound. Other studies have found that new parents forming a group can be very helpful. As we saw in Chapter 3, the first child can change the lives of its parents dramatically. Many find that they become quite distanced from their old and still childless friends as a result, which can lead to much resentment. A group gives new contact and again helps people understand their experience. A very healthy recent trend is the many self-help groups springing up for just this supportive purpose. Alcoholics Anonymous has had the idea for many years but now former mental patients, people preparing for marriage, single parents and others are banding together for a similar purpose.

The limited data available suggest that a particularly useful type of network to have in order to better cope with stress appears to be a fairly loose one, although this may not be true for everyone. A looser network gives one access to a variety of different contacts, different types of people. So, as one's needs and interests change with time, as they inevitably must, one is more likely to find people to meet them, or even find a soulmate. This was suggested by a recent study of two sets of women, all over thirty years old, by Hirsch (1980). They were going through some major life crisis. Some had just been widowed and others were shedding their housewife role of many years to return to full-time university study. So much change was afoot, and much re-adjustment necessary. The study found that those with loose-knit networks usually fared much better in the struggle to cope. Most successful of all were those whose relationships with members of their networks were multiplex.

Since just about all of us need a sound network, the next question is how to go about creating one, or extending our present one. This can be a problem for many, for a variety of reasons. Some difficulties are that we all differ considerably in our need for contact, our sociability, our attractiveness to others and our skills at making friends. Some of us just naturally are better at these and thus more likely to have a large network.

Perhaps the first place to start is to try to improve the quality of the contacts one already has. Try to deepen relation-ships, make single ones multiplex, extend their basis in other directions. Nudge yourself in this direction to make just a little more effort. Every now and again someone starts up a campaign to try to get us to do just that: such as the "Have you hugged your kid today?" one.

A network can be extended in several ways. First of all one can join voluntary organizations, clubs and hobby groups and so on. Also, more and more self-help groups form for people going through a particular crisis, as we saw above. These can often be learned about from the telephone book. Try to use your existing contacts to develop new branches to your network. Many people report that that is the more effective way. However, one major barrier can make it very hard for particular individuals to form a network. This is a lack of good social skills, to which we now turn.

SOCIAL SKILLS

The last section showed how important having a sound network can be. Without one, or with a weak one, one's stress level may be much higher and one's ability to cope with crises much weakened. Nevertheless, so many people still end up with small, non-supportive or even non-existent networks, essentially alone and friendless. Why? For some it is inclination. They are naturally loners, preferring their own company to others'. For a great many others, the problem lies in interaction skills, social skills which need to be polished up. The power to interact well is a skill, one that gets better with knowledge and practice, just as is the ability to cope well or to play tennis well. As with other skills, some are just naturally quicker to learn but virtually everyone can. With much practice, social skills become practically automatic, as does driving a car. The suave diplomat or chief of protocol has a long history of experience behind him.

Yet another reason is that some people will not conform to certain groups' mores, or find it very difficult to. Every group demands some conformity, demands that its members act and think somewhat alike. To stay accepted in some groups, one might have to be interested in Bach and Mozart, wear the very latest fashions and drive a Porsche. Joining a juvenile street gang in the Bronx might require carrying a switchblade knife (and using it), swearing a lot, and intensely disliking the forces of law and order. This principle of groups demanding conformity, even supposedly groups for nonconformists, was well illustrated by a cartoon from the 1960s. It showed two trios walking past each other. One trio was the "straight" stereotype of the time: clean-shaven, crew-cut, wearing neat conservative clothes. The other trio consisted of the nonconformists of the time: beatniks wearing old jeans, weird shirts and beards. But the funny point was that all three in each group looked identical. Even the nonconformists conformed, just to a different drummer.

Some conformity is necessary for any group. No group can survive long unless there is some working together. There must be some rules for how to act, and most people must pretty closely follow them. Anyone who flaunts the rules too much usually is punished in some way, or if too many violate them, the group disintegrates. And of course, there often is great conflict between an individual's aims and needs and those of the group. Literature is full of works on this theme: the individual fighting the group — whether to give up some individual freedom and conform or suffer isolation and loneliness.

Let us now look more closely at social skills. Just what does it mean to be socially skilled? Michael Argyle, an Oxford psychologist and a pioneer in this area, gives one definition. He sees it as the ability to affect others as you want in a way that is socially acceptable. So, it is the talent to persuade a friend to go on a date, the boss to try out your new idea, your spouse to make some changes or concessions about the household, to get others in a group you have just joined to accept and like you. And this action is done in a way that others see as positive: by persuasion and cajoling, not by threats or coercion. Having good social skills requires a vast knowledge about what to do in particular circumstances, how best to respond to certain types of people, and requires a good sense of timing. This knowledge ranges from something trivial like the correct fork to pick up at dinner, to all the steps required in courtship, to the ability to convince an interviewer that you are the right person for the job.

A socially unskilled person usually appears to others as inept, cold and unrewarding, uninteresting and perhaps even annoying, and thus not a person they wish to keep interacting with and often whom they may begin to politely avoid. Here are a

82

few case examples of some people low on social skills.

One of the prevalent stereotypes in our society is the incompetent bachelor male. We can feel desperately sorry for him as he struggles along in a vain, anxious attempt to impress some girl or get her to go out with him. His movements may be very jerky and he keeps saying the wrong thing, perhaps not understanding the courtship rituals or women well enough to succeed, or failing through too much anxiety. American comedian Woody Allen frequently portrays such a character in his movies.

Another prevalent stereotype is the person with few inter-action skills at all. Such a person may just not know how to begin and end conversations with strangers, how to reward others enough to keep a conversation going. Such people are often mis-perceived. They get seen as not necessarily just unskilled but as arrogant (especially if physically attractive), anti-social or simply disinterested in others. An extreme social deficit along these lines can eventually land a person in a mental institution.

A third stereotype is the unfortunate person stuck some-where in the lower rungs of a corporation or some other large organization. They may be particularly good at their jobs but for some reason do not get on well with superiors and so do not advance. Working day after day in a tense social atmosphere can be very stressful. Jack Vance once wrote a vastly amusing science-fiction story about such a person, called "Dodkin's Job". The hero started off high in the organization but sunk lower and lower (to Class D/flunky/unskilled) because he was too bright, too independent, sarcastic and stubborn to play the games necessary to succeed. These included being extremely gregarious with the bosses, working hard and enthusiastically, working overtime and so on. In this case, he knew what to do but his stubborn character stopped him doing it. But events turned out well for the hero. He discovered that the organization was really run from a tiny office way down in the cellars and adroitly manoeuvred himself into this job.

Certain persons may appear socially unskilled because they have trouble in just a couple of types of situation. Perhaps the most common is dating and courtship. Others may be dealing with superiors, or negotiating with a spouse. There are not much data on the prevalence of such skill deficits, but one study of students in England is suggestive. It suggested that about nine per cent of students experience significant stress in social situations.

Over time, a chronic lack of skills can lead to a number of disorders. First, an unskilled person is likely to become very isolated. Isolation itself can lead to all sorts of problems (and is very stressful for most, which is why prisons use solitary confinement as punishment). It can lead to very disordered thinking, partly because there is no check from others on the validity of one's ideas. One can even start to believe that the CIA or KGB are in hot pursuit, or that Earth will soon be invaded from Mars. Also, continual rebuffs from others can lead to great frustration and bitter feelings towards humanity in general. A major historical force in our time is the "crazed" loner who kills a major statesman or hijacks a plane, usually for some sound (to him) reason. In the person's distorted view of the world, such actions may seem perfectly reasonable.

Another common result of a social-skills deficit is depression. Too little human contact can quickly lead to depression, which in turn produces a vicious cycle. Most people find depressed persons pretty tedious company (they talk little, and promote a very pessimistic view of events and the future) and so start to avoid them. This leads to more isolation and more depression which creates yet more isolation. For some, this continuing abyss can seem bottomless. Indeed, numerous studies have shown that people particularly prone to depression tend to have fewer social skills.

Yet another result of isolation (and perhaps its cause in some cases) is alienation. Here a person seems to have no strong links to any social groups, no significant ties to others, and does not accept many values of the society in which he or she lives. Thus he may be unsure who he is and what values he holds. The present-day world, with its weakening of traditional values and of religion's influence, promotion of the idea of cultural relativism, and high rate of social change may make this syndrome more prevalent.

To understand what can go wrong in a person's handling of social situations (and lead to the above syndromes), we first need to look at the elements of skilled social behavior. Much research has been done on this topic in the last decade or so and a good notion of its basics is developing. The research has been carried out in a number of disciplines; from sociologists and anthropologists studying human communication to ethologists examining the social interactions of birds, fish, and humans. Much of this work has been put together into a model by Michael Argyle and his colleagues (for example, Trower, Bryant and Argyle, 1978) and I make much use of it in the next few pages.

The latter authors note a few major points about interactions. First, people usually have a clear goal in mind when interacting with another. They are talking for a reason and they know what that reason is. They interact to attain it. It may simply be to catch up on the latest gossip, to further worm into the good graces of the boss, to settle a dispute, or just to talk to someone to relieve loneliness. To achieve such goals, usually both parties have a set of rules laid down by society that must be more or less followed. Thus the rules for getting a girl to go out for the evening are usually based on persuasion, cajoling, friendliness, and so on. Grabbing her by the hair and dragging her along or threatening to burn down her house is definitely out. In trying to gain their goals, participants generally try to pick up cues about what the other is thinking and feeling, how he or she is reacting to what they say and do. One's behavior then is tailored to the other's reactions. For example, if person A continually swears and talks about sex and then sees person B wince each time, A generally cuts both out. Similarly, if person A's conversation topic appears to be sending person B into slumberland, A usually switches topics until he finds one that interests B. Two persons typically are in some synchrony when they interact, taking turns doing the actual talking and deftly picking up the lead, filling in pauses when the other person falters.

People skilled at interaction also use a variety of techniques to keep a conversation going smoothly. First, when appropriate they tend to ask questions, either to get another to further elaborate on what was said, or as a filler to stop the conversation lapsing. Second, they tend to use statements that are easy to reply to. Unskilled people, on the other hand, often drop conversation stoppers — statements which leave one person at a loss for a response.

Much interaction takes place to a fixed sequence. Argyle calls them routines, but they could also be called scripts. For example, consider the routine of casually greeting an acquaintance hurrying in one direction while you hurry in another. It might go like this ... "Hi, how are you?" "Fine, and you?" "Pretty good, but I will be even better when I get this assignment done." "OK, nice to see you, but must rush for my appointment." The people involved may vary the words to some extent, but the rules of the interaction are prescribed. We have many, many such routines, from the steps involved in eating in a restaurant, introducing one friend to another, to ending an interaction. Just as important as knowing the many routines is giving feedback. Two skilled people interacting smile and nod at each other. They also carefully pay attention to what the other says, and try to appear interested in it.

Much research has made it clear that a very large part of human communication is non-verbal. What we actually say, the content of our speech, is only part of the story. How we say it (that is, sarcastically, enthusiastically), our tone, voice intensity, amount of eye contact, posture, position of limbs and even the distance you sit from another all communicate much. For example, a person who gives little eye contact, sits facing away, and talks tonelessly usually communicates dislike or disinterest. A person who rocks back on his chair, looks relaxed, has his hands behind his head, or has asymmetrical limb positions usually communicates that he feels superior to whomever he is talking to. A boss about to give an errant employee a dressing-down might look that way. A whole range of messages is given by dress, style, grooming and other appearance factors. Particular parts of the body tend to communicate certain things. Emotion, for example, tends to be communicated in the face and hands. While most of us learn to disguise or hide facial expressions, the hands often are harder to control. Thus an anxious person's face may look serene but his active hands may betray his true feelings.

What then can go wrong? What sorts of mistakes do unskilled people typically make to destroy the harmony of their interactions?

One is a lack of thought in social situations, which we cover in more detail in Chapter 11. Some other frequent errors are suggested by the above analysis of normal social interaction. Unskilled persons tend to have no goals or very vague ones in an interaction. Many are not very rewarding to others, they don't provide enough smiles, nods, agreement and attention. Many do not know enough interaction routines or do not know them well enough. As well, unskilled people often do not vary their behavior enough across situations and people. They are too consistent, too unaccommodating, they do not bend with the differing norms and rules governing different situations. Another very common fault of the unskilled is too much self-absorption. They appear too self-centred, too disinterested in others to make others wish to interact. Disinterest is usually rapidly reciprocated. While most of us of course are guilty of some self-absorption (Ambrose Bierce in *The Devil's Dictionary* satirically defined "self" as "the most important person in the universe"), one can still go overboard. This can also mean being too self-centred to take another's point of view, being unable to step into his shoes. One's own perspectives and ways are seen as the only correct ones.

This fault can bedevil cross-cultural interactions. Sometimes a person from one culture tries to impose his own rules and values on someone from another. The result is usually disaster from numerous misunderstandings. One common example is in bargaining. In the East, hardly any prices are fixed and the buyer and seller may haggle for hours over one. Since Westerners are usually seen as immensely wealthy, the prices generally are hiked for them. Many take this as an attempt to cheat them and yell and scream, get very angry and may walk off in a huff. (Others are almost as bad, they pay the first price asked and drive the overall price structure skyward.) The typical seller usually cannot understand all this fuss. The best way is to treat the whole situation as a game. The exorbitant first price has to be smiled at; you laugh, cajole, tell the seller how poor you are and how many meals you will have to miss to buy the object. When you get to a price from which he apparently will not budge, you point out the object's defects and how much cheaper it is elsewhere. Then you can even walk away, to possibly be called back and quoted a lower price.

Much can go wrong in the non-verbal domain. People may be thinking and feeling one thing but communicate another through faulty signals. For example, too much inhibition due to social anxiety can be misinterpreted as arrogance or dislike and disinterest. Someone may also have an expression that is too negative, even when his thoughts do not match it. He may therefore be seen as sarcastic, superior, and not at all friendly. A person may learn the wrong display rules. In other words, he may feel friendly and wish to show it to a female friend but somehow comes across as lecherous.

Some social-skill deficits occur in a cluster, a set. One very common one is lack of *assertiveness*. Non-assertive people do not stand up for themselves is many situations, do not ask quite reasonable requests of friends, and yet comply with quite unreasonable ones from others. Thus their rights are often trampled on. Often the problem is not that the person lacks the will or the knowledge to be assertive, just that he or she is just too inhibited.

The above discussion gives some idea of the many social-skill deficits that exist. It is well beyond the scope of this book to detail much of what is now known about human interaction, what can go wrong, and how to improve one's skills. That task would take a very large volume in itself. But, here are a few major ways to improve social skills.

First, read some of the many books on non-verbal communication. Because such a truly astounding amount is communicated by subtleties of posture, voice tone and facial expression, one can much better improve one's understanding of others and power to communicate by learning them. Second, monitor your own behavior and that of others. Look for and give feedback, try to convey interest and likeability, even if you do not always feel it. Generally our social faces are quite different from our real ones, anyway. Experiment with new ways of behaving, try out new strategies which you can rehearse (either mentally or actually) before taking the plunge. Finally, always try to have a clear goal in any interaction. Know what you want to achieve and work to achieve it.

CHAPTER 6

Individual Differences

Lefcourt (1980) tells an inspiring story about a middle-aged man
he calls Richard X, a true titan in the struggle to cope with
adversity. For a long time there was barely a cloud in this man's
sky. He owned a manufacturing company, had a loving wife and
children, and flew his own light plane all over the USA. But, one
fateful day he crashed while taking off, killing a passenger, and
his life thereafter took a distinct downturn. Months of hospital
followed. He lost an eye, had many bones shattered, needed
plastic surgery and even came down with ulcers and pneumonia.
These injuries caused him much pain. But, over time and with
very little encouragement from his nurses, he forced himself to
recover. He slowly regained use of hands and limbs. Just a year
after the crash, though wired together in many places, he had
returned to most of his normal work and life activities. He looked
forward to flying again, to buying another plane, and to building
a new house. Richard X recovered rapidly from a horrendously
stressful experience which would have permanently floored many
others. Other examples of good copers with adversity we saw in
Chapter 4, from the fictional one in *The Deerhunter* to the real-
life survivors of concentration and prisoner-of-war camps.

At the other end of this spectrum of stress resistance are
the many who cannot seem to cope well with their circumstances.
A minor life change or a temporary crisis may seem to overwhelm
them, sending them into great anxiety or depression.

There are indeed wide individual differences in the
tolerance that different people have to stress. One striking
example is from a study by Hamburg, Hamburg and DeGoza
(1953) of people showing great variation in their reactions to a
similar stressor, severe burns:

*When a psychiatric observer enters a ward in which there are a
number of severely burned patients, all in the acute phase
(covered with bandages, receiving transfusions and so on), he
is likely to be impressed by the varieties of behaviors evident.
One patient is crying, moaning, complaining, demanding that
more be done for him; another appears completely comfortable
and unconcerned; another appears intensely preoccupied and
seems to make very little contact with the observer; still
another appears sad and troubled but friendly, responding
with a weak smile to any approach made to him; and so it goes
from one bed to the next.*

Why do these individual differences in resistance to stress
and the ability to cope with it occur? Or, to ask a broader
question, why do some people seem to lead much more stressful
lives, having difficulty dealing with the stressors they face?

Part of the answer of course is just luck. Some people are
seemingly born blessed; with physical attractiveness that makes
their lives smoother, with charm, wealth and social status, or with
living in a historically safe place and time. These will usually
reduce the number of stressors they must face and give many
resources to tackle those they cannot avoid.

But the above is only part of the answer. Much of the rest
of it lies elsewhere; in factors like age, sex and cultural origin, in
basic personality traits, differing early experiences, different
temperaments, mental attitudes and knowledge of stress and
coping. In this chapter we examine some of these in turn to try to
account for the wide individual differences in stress resistance.
Then we examine some studies of particularly effective copers,
people like Richard X, to see what personal qualities may be useful in good coping.

INDIVIDUAL DIFFERENCES IN TOTAL
STRESS FACED

Some people find it easy to cope with their circumstances because
they do not face as much stress as others. There can be various
reasons for this. Their personalities and temperaments may mean

they encounter fewer stressors and respond less to those they do face, for example. Let us look at such factors in more detail.

BASIC PERSONALITY TRAITS   One way to look at personality is to see it as consisting of many traits; ones like dominance, independence, extroversion, rigidity, and so on. These suggest some consistency in the way a person high on a certain trait behaves across situations. For example, a person high on dominance might be dominant at home, at work with subordinates, and in various social groups.

Having particular basic traits in certain circumstances may predispose a person to more stress. Let us take an extreme hypothetical example to illustrate; say a highly stubborn Russian dissident with a well-developed moral sense. Say that he continually criticizes the Soviet political system for its injustices, despite loss of job, ostracism, threats and exile to Siberia. The continual harassment by authorities will constitute a continuous series of stressors. If he were less stubborn and accepted things as they were, most of these stressors would disappear. True, his conscience might then become a source of stress, but perhaps not as great as that the State dished out.

As other examples, in certain societies a particular trait might mean success and social acceptance but much flak and stress in another. A pushy, aggressive manner might be an asset in the USA but definitely would be much less of one in an Eastern culture like Thailand or Japan. Rigidity is a final example. In our rather changeable world, some flexibility and bending with the wind is usually needed. An overly rigid person may not continually adjust his or her thinking and actions as circumstances alter and a failure to so bend may mean more stress.

A much-studied personality difference which leaves people in the wrong category more stress-prone is the Type A and Type B distinction. Type As have a great sense of time urgency; they must get as much done as fast as possible. They are driven to succeed in life, to strive for prestige and material goods, to be very competitive. They can become very frustrated when their path to goals is thwarted. They try to hurry others up, sometimes finishing sentences for conversation partners. They find it hard to relax, hard to do anything but work. Type Bs have much less sense of time urgency and are not so striving and materialistic.

91

They can easily relax, and are much more flexible and open to learning.

Type As seem to be much more prone to at least one stress-related illness, heart disease. Evidently, this is because they face more stress simply because of their driven nature. A tennis game, for example, might be a pleasant, relaxing diversion for a B but a hard, competitive battle for an A that he or she desperately must win.

On the other side of this coin are traits that may lessen the amount of stress. Some we just saw in the Type Bs; flexibility, lack of competitiveness, and the power to relax. Certain abilities may also reduce one's life stressors. One clear example is probably intelligence. One might expect the more intelligent to better anticipate stress sources and act to counter them, to better be able to think through and solve problems. Also here are social, communication and negotiation abilities.

TEMPERAMENT DIFFERENCES   A temperament is a disposition, a tendency to respond in a certain way with a certain force. Willerman (1979) describes three generally recognized major ones. The first is *activity*, how energetic one appears. The second is *sociability*, how much one needs and wishes the company of others. The third, and perhaps most important here, is *emotionality*. This is how quickly and easily one becomes emotionally aroused, how readily the stress response is set off by events. People low on emotionality seem to be upset by many fewer events, do not react with as much force to them, and habituate quickly. Their mood tends to be much more even. At the opposite end are the highly emotional, who respond quickly and with much force to many events. They take much time to habituate to such stressors, and many do not seem to habituate to some at all. Their mood may be very uneven, rapidly switching from mild elation to depression seemingly at the drop of a hat.

While these basic temperaments may be much modified by child-rearing and other kinds of experience, they seem to have a strong genetic basis. Nurses say that newborn babies differ greatly in their activity and emotionality levels, for example. Scientists can easily breed rats or mice for emotionality. Dogs have already been so bred. The Saint Bernard, for example, is a quiet, placid, mild-mannered animal while the German shepherd or Doberman Pinscher can be readily trained to kill.

It seems clear that a highly emotional temperament will predispose a given person to a more stressful life. There will be more events to react to, the stress reaction to them may be longer and stronger, and it will persist because they take more time to habituate. As well, a more sociable temperament may be a plus in securing social resources to aid in weathering stressors.

DIFFERENCES IN PRIOR EXPERIENCES We saw in Chapter 4 how traumatic experiences, such as combat or imprisonment in a concentration camp, can lead to a post-traumatic stress syndrome which persists well into the future. Childhood experiences may also leave a person more vulnerable to certain sorts of stressors as an adult. An early trauma may leave a psychological scar that never really heals. Thus a person may react to certain events as great stressors, ones which leave others unmoved. For example, an individual might have a boating accident in which he or she nearly drowned. Thereafter boats and ships and anything to do with travelling on water might be stress-inducing.

Janis (1971) calls this phenomenon *sensitization*, where a person exposed to actual danger becomes much more sensitive to later similar signs of threat. He mentions studies of sport parachutists which demonstrated it experimentally. The first leap from a plane gives most jumpers an overwhelming feeling of terror, which may take much time to recover from. Epstein and Fenz showed that jumpers reacted much more emotionally to words that had anything to do with leaping out of aeroplanes after that first jump.

DIFFERENCES IN APPRAISAL Another factor making for individual differences is variation in the two phases of the stress/coping process; in primary and secondary appraisal. Let us consider secondary appraisal first, which was described in Chapter 1, a calculation of whether one's coping powers are up to handling an imminent stressor. This may determine whether the stressor is seen as an interesting challenge or an impending disaster to be somehow survived. Since we differ greatly in coping skills and resources, total amount of stress should differ as well, therefore, due to secondary appraisal differences.

Variations in primary appraisal also should have a

significant impact. We differ greatly in the events that we perceive as stressors. While the truly intense ones (like natural disasters and imprisonment) are likely to be stressful to everyone, milder events are not.

One factor that can make some events stressors to one person but not to another is misperception, a topic covered in much greater detail in Chapter 10. Because of particular ways of thinking, or not understanding given situations well enough, one person may see threats and danger where there really is none. Another factor is motivation. All of us differ considerably in our social motives and evidently in the strength of our biological ones as well. Sex for example, is much more important to some people than others. Some have a strong need for power, for success, social status, material wealth, for security and stability. So a given event might be a great threat to one person, frustrating his important goals, but not to someone else without such motives.

This was shown by Mahl (1949). He interviewed eight students about to take an exam to determine their entrance to medical school, an important possible challenge to their career goals. Six were quite stressed by the impending test, according to a physiological measure, but two were not. Why? One had already been accepted to a good medical school, so the exam was no threat to his goals at all. The other was calm because his motivation to do well academically was very low. He had little real desire for advanced study and so his weak motivation also meant the exam was no threat to his future goals. Again, this goes back to the definition of stress given in Chapter 1. For an event to be stressful, resolving it must matter to us in some way.

INDIVIDUAL DIFFERENCES IN COPING METHODS

People have different preferred methods of coping with stressors. At a broad level, some prefer to directly attack sources of stress, others to avoid or escape them. We saw in earlier chapters the quite dramatically different extreme ways in which people may cope; from hysteria and multiple personality to obsessive-compulsive rituals. People also prefer different defence

94

mechanisms as well. Some typically use repression and denial, and others rationalization. Indeed, a person's characteristic ways of dealing with stressors are an intrinsic part of his or her personality. And since, according to circumstances, given coping methods will vary in success, this also should mean wide individual differences in ability to withstand stress.

QUALITIES OF EFFECTIVE COPERS

What exactly is a good coper? We might expect one to be a person able to minimize the number of stress sources in his or her life and to anticipate and handle well those that must be faced. And thus one would expect such a person to have low levels of emotional distress, for his or her circumstances, anyway.

There have been a number of studies of apparently good copers and we describe a few of these here. Our major concern here is to try to determine what qualities seem most useful in the battle to deal with adversity. We look in particular at two such qualities. One is a basic personality trait; locus of control. The other is a mental attitude; a sense of mastery, a belief in self-efficacy, a feeling that one will ultimately triumph over life's vicissitudes.

An early study of good copers was carried out by Grinker (1962). He examined some male students at a college in Chicago who appeared to be well-adjusted from their scores on psychological tests. In-depth interviews suggested that these men were free of any disabling, neurotic traits, on the surface at any rate. Their school performances were about average. But the most striking things about them were their general contentment with their lives and circumstances and their conforming nature. Mainly they wanted to do their jobs well, "To do well, to do good, and to be liked". Grinker said that none of them was likely to make any great impact on society. They had little ambition, little will to rise in society and make a lot of money. They present a great contrast to the hordes of frustrated, striving people who live stressful lives partly because of a constant wish to do better, to acquire more status and possessions. Some of the most stress-prone seem to be those willing to readily shift to a new city or job for some salary or status advance, and to continually be frustrated when such goals are not quickly met.

A not completely dissimilar portrait of good copers comes from a mammoth series of studies summarized by Hinkle (1973). A variety of different groups were looked at for their overall health; Americans working in unchanging environments, refugees from Hungary and China and ex-political prisoners. The groups had undergone much stress, through persecution, great change, or the sheer lack of change. Yet there were enormous differences in the effects on their physical and mental well-being of all this turmoil. Those who coped particularly well seemed remarkably alike:

> ... the healthiest members of our samples often showed little psychological reaction to events and situations which caused profound reactions in other members of the group. The loss of a husband or wife, the separation from one's family, the isolation from one's friends, community, or country, the frustration of apparently important desires, or the failure to attain apparently important goals produced no profound or lasting reaction. They seemed to have a shallow attachment to people, goals, or groups, and they readily shifted to other relationships when established relationships were disrupted. There was an almost "sociopathic" flavor to some of them. Others endured prolonged deprivations, boredom or sustained hard work without obvious adverse effects.

> Many of these people displayed a distinct awareness of their own limitations and their physiological needs. They behaved as if their own well-being were one of their primary concerns. They avoided situations that would make demands on them if they felt they could not, or did not want to meet these demands. An employed man or woman might refuse a promotion because he did not want the increased responsibility, refuse a transfer because it was "too much trouble", or refuse to work overtime because it might be too tiring — despite the fact that each of these changes might have increased his income, increased his prestige, or increased his opportunity to get ahead in his occupation. As family members, such people might refuse to take the responsibility for an aged or ill parent or sibling, giving as an explanation a

statement implying that it would be "too much for me". If such a person learned that family members or relatives in a foreign country were in need, or were being oppressed, he might give little evidence of concern about this, and he might explain, if asked, that he saw no reason to worry about it since there was nothing he could do about it. If it was to be the lot in life of such a person to be poor, or to live alone, he seemed to feel no need to be unhappy about this or to rebel against it. Such psychological characteristics, and the attitudes that accompanied them, appear to play a role in the "immunity" of some people to the effects of deprivation and change. [Hinkle, 1973.]

The above two groups seemed to cope effectively partly through insulation, through a passive attitude. But other good copers may present quite a different personality picture. Ruff and Korchin (1964) examined the seven astronauts in the Mercury space programme of the early 1960s, seeing them as unusually competent and healthy men, well able to handle stress. Tom Wolfe in *The Right Stuff* also describes them. They had all been military test pilots, a dangerous occupation if ever there was one, and one that needs recruits well able to handle stress. Korchin and Ruff found that these astronauts indeed had very good control over their emotions. They believed strongly in their ability to master stress and situations. When in a tight spot they would try not to become unduly emotional, would stop and assess the circumstances, decide what must be done and then proceed to do just that.

All had grown up in small towns or on farms, places where they gained a firm sense of who they were. They had grown up in security, had identified strongly with their fathers, and were largely free from the haunting self-doubts that plague many others. They were very ambitious and highly motivated. Their lives had generally been quite smooth, having few crises, with easy transitions between phases.

One feature that stands out is the astronauts' sense of mastery, of faith in their ability to overcome obstacles. The case of Richard X at this chapter's start shows much the same thing, which Lefcourt calls a sense of "can-ness", a faith that one *can* deal with events effectively. This sense of self-efficacy has been much talked about by many writers but was elaborated into a more explicit theory by Bandura (1977). He argues that this sense of mastery is critical to coping, and is a major determinant of individual differences in coping ability. He even goes on to say that any procedure that helps people cope better (from relaxation training through to psychotherapy) works because it enhances the belief in self-efficacy. First the principle will be described in more detail.

Bandura argues that a need to master our environment is a basic human motivator (see also Goldfried and Robins, 1982). We strive for a sense of competence, a belief that we can weather events like shifts in job, residence, divorce, setbacks and dashing of hopes and still come out on top, and generally deal well with the world. This sense of self-efficacy is extremely important in coping for several reasons, argues Bandura. First, it will determine whether one tries at all to cope with a particular stressor. A person with little belief in his or her self-efficacy may not try. A stressor like the loss of a job may pack much more punch if a person sees himself as without the skills and persuasiveness to go out and get another one and so does not even try.

Second, the sense of mastery may affect how hard one tries to cope with stressors. Again, a person who believes that he or she will ultimately overcome some adversity may mobilize many more coping resources; gathering as much information as possible, seeking help and advice from others, and trying many different approaches and coping methods. A person with a low sense of mastery who sees himself as destined to fail anyway may not try anywhere near so hard, perhaps also lapsing early into a state of learned helplessness.

Third, the mastery sense may affect how long one persists in trying. Again, a believer in ultimate triumph is not likely to give up easily or early, keeping on until he or she succeeds. One can see this difference in belief in self sometimes in sports tournaments. Some players when they get well behind in a match often seem to virtually give up, fighting on only half-heartedly. Others, however, seem to play at their best when down, still believing they will ultimately win if they only try harder.

Such a sense of self-efficacy may not, however, extend to every sphere of life except perhaps for a few very fortunate and favored individuals. Thus a person may see himself as very efficacious in one area (such as selling encyclopaedias, or all work matters) but very inefficacious in others (such as love or in dealing with subordinates).

How does one develop a sense of mastery in a given sphere? Bandura argues that there are four major sources of experience that may shape one. The first of these is quite obvious; consistent success in dealing with events. Repeated success should help build up a sense of mastery and repeated failure should lower it. Many successes should lead to a strong sense which occasional failures will barely dent. The second is from watching others succeed. For example, if a person has a mild phobia of all snakes and sees someone else readily handle one, that may increase the belief that he himself can successfully handle them too.

A third source is persuasion by others. Here a person may actively try to convince another that he really can do something, really can handle a particular stressor. Bandura says this method is not as effective as the above two because one or two failures afterward may wipe out the new belief in mastery. Nothing helps as much as experience. The final source is emotional arousal. Bandura points out that we may use the extent to which we become emotional in a given situation as a measure of success in dealing with it. For example, if one becomes very anxious at a job interview one can see this as evidence of inefficacy at job interviews. So, if one gets much practice at relaxation training and anticipation of interview questions, subsequent low anxiety at the next one may be interpreted as mastery of the situation.

Closely related to the sense of mastery is a very important dimension along which people differ; locus of control. People are thought to differ in how much they believe that events in the world are under the control of their own efforts. At one extreme are "externals". They see themselves as having little or no control over their environment. Their locus of control is in the external world. They see themselves more at the mercy of fate, of chance, of the whims of others. "Internals" are at the other end. They believe just the opposite; that many events are within the control of the individual, that there is much a person can do to affect his or her fate. Being an "internal" is not quite the same as having a sense of mastery, however, as Bandura points out. One can have this strong belief but have no coping skills and thus see oneself as inefficacious.

Lefcourt (1980) suggests that internals are more likely to succeed at coping with life's adversities. The belief that events are potentially controllable may do much to lessen stress. The sense of "can-ness", as in the case of Richard X, may mean one overcomes many of life's adversities by an active effort. But, a caution is needed here. An internal locus of control may not be adaptive for all stressors and situations. As we saw in Chapters 2 and 3, some stressors are best met with philosophical resignation. But a strong "internal" may keep trying to find ways to bring a basically uncontrollable stressor under control. Like Don Quixote, they may expend much effort and suffer much frustration on an essentially hopeless quest.

PART II

PART II

CHAPTER 7

Physical Exercise as an Active Coping Technique

The mind is easily affected by a number of purely physical factors, from drugs and diet to fatigue. Our ability to withstand stress in large part depends on how well we watch what happens to our bodies. Stress may take more toll when the body is weakened; by poor diet, too much sugar, too little sleep, too many drugs, and so on. Just as a social network can act as a stress insulator, so may sound diet and enough sleep, for example. (Further information on this topic is given by Shaffer, 1982.)

Such purely physical factors may be a direct cause of faulty adjustment, or at least its symptoms. Many hyperactive children, for example, seem to be overactive because of allergies to certain food additives. Their symptoms may disappear when they go on a special diet. Another similar and very common but little-recognized ailment is caffeinism; addiction to the stimulant drug present in coffee, tea, chocolate, cocoa and cola drinks. Some people are very sensitive to caffeine and everyday doses can lead to symptoms of anxiety; tremors, nervousness, insomnia, irritability, and even paranoia. People have turned up to psychologists' offices complaining of such ills and wondering what purely psychological factor is causing them. Often their onset is traced to their buying a coffee percolator, which delivers much stronger amounts of caffeine per cup than does instant. A few days off caffeine and the symptoms may completely vanish. It is not yet known how many such ailments will ultimately be traced to chemicals.

Another physical factor that affects one's power to resist stress is physical exercise. Regular workouts can have a number of positive effects in the struggle to cope effectively. When not physically fit, one may have much less resistance to stressors and so they pack more punch. A bout of regular exercise is itself a stressor and so may help to inoculate against other ones. And, as we will see, physical exercise is an excellent palliative, an active way of working on the symptoms of stress.

First we give some perspective on physical fitness; what it is, why it is so important and then look at its merits in detail.

PHYSICAL FITNESS

They become visible in the early morning and evening. They huff and puff through the streets and fields, strain up and coast down hills. They have been a familiar sight since the jogging craze took hold.

Runners are just the tip of the back-to-fitness iceberg. Many once sedentary people now are doing their best to become fit. Swimming pools are filled with swimmers doing lap after mechanical lap, roads and parks swarm with bicycle riders, and callisthenic classes have started up everywhere. Even one of the most exacting and painful sports of all, weight-lifting, is gathering new disciples.

The fitness boom has been noted and praised in many books and countless magazine articles. These have pointed out two important benefits which help explain why so many have become converts. One is the most obvious — loss of weight. Because of the vast mountain of food present in most Western nations, many of us are doing what we are biologically programmed to do — eating more than we really need. As a result, many get overweight. But, despite the numerous crash and fad diets published every week, the battle of the bulge is usually lost from the start without exercise. Neither diets nor the typical psychological methods of weight control really help. As A. J. Stunkard put it:

Most obese persons will not stay in treatment for obesity. Of those who do stay in treatment, most will not lose weight, and of those who do lose weight, most will regain it.

Indeed, some scientists believe that we are each more-or-less genetically set to have a certain amount of fat given that we can eat all we want. If our intake falls below that level, we start to feel ravenously hungry and ultimately crack if dieting. The only way this set-point can be changed, they argue, is by exercise. Regular workouts speed up the rate at which one uses up calories, for many hours afterward. And it converts more of the body to muscle rather than fat, muscle needing more calories to be maintained.

The other much-talked-about benefit of physical fitness is better physical health. Fit people have more of a glow, more of a get-up-and-go attitude, and are much less prone to certain physical ailments and diseases, in particular those of the heart. One study in England, for example, found that people who walked to work (for more than twenty minutes each way) had a significantly smaller chance of coming down with heart disease later in life than those who did not. Another famous study in the 1950s looked at London bus drivers and conductors. Their backgrounds were very similar — they lived in the same neighborhoods, and had the same education levels and lifestyles. But, the amount of exercise they got was very different. The driver sat for most of the day while the conductor chased about; running to get to particular passengers before they got off, clambering up and down the stairs of the famous double-decker buses and so on. The study found that the more active conductors had a much smaller risk of heart disease than the drivers.

And recently, scientists have begun to note a third benefit; that exercise helps the mind as much as the body. Exercise may help us better adapt to the stresses and strains of our environment.

Let us just digress for a moment for some historical perspective on fitness. Up until the end of the nineteenth century most of humanity worked as farmers. Only this century, at least in the industrialized nations of the West, have most people shifted to sedentary jobs and lifestyles. Now, farm work is hard — very hard. You have to get up early in the morning and often go on until sundown. There is always something that has to be done. Often a farmer works seven days a week, especially at harvest time. I will never forget the month or so that a friend and I worked as fruitpickers on the South Island of New Zealand. We had to work hard and fast because we were paid by how much we picked. The crack of dawn would find us on top of ladders, bending this way and that. At night we were so physically tired that all we wanted to do was sleep, which took all of about thirty seconds to achieve. There was no insomnia on that farm. But for all this, we felt good; physically and mentally good. We had no room for anxiety and depression, the common complaints of our sedentary society.

Indeed, the change in Western lifestyles from active to sedentary may be one reason why stress and stress-related disorders really take their toll, why anxiety and depression seem so much more widespread. Our early ancestors also had many stressors to worry about; whether there would be enough food to survive the winter, whether any of the killer diseases later generations have conquered would strike. Further back in time, people had to worry about whether their city or town would be sacked this year by more powerful neighbors, the men being killed and the women and children sold as slaves. Life was also much shorter — life expectancy being only thirty or forty years on average. Yet, perhaps partly because they were so much more physically active, stress did not seem to be such a problem.

Exercise physiologists usually distinguish between three main types of fitness. The first is the weight-lifter's sheer muscular strength. The second type is joint flexibility, gained from bending and stretching exercises. But the third and most important type is *cardiovascular*, the fitness of the heart.

This is simply the ability of the heart to pump oxygen to the parts of the body that need it during exercise. Whole-body exercises such as running or swimming increase the overall physical need for oxygen. When the heart is fit, it has no trouble providing it. But an unfit heart cannot deliver and so a person stops, out of breath, and if he has pushed himself too hard, may even faint.

Regular whole-body exercises that get the heart beating faster make it more adept at pumping oxygen. Indeed, athletes who work out all day, day in and day out, may over time develop a larger heart (and a bigger appetite) to handled this physical demand.

But the reverse also occurs. A few weeks of our usual sedentary lifestyle with its elevators, escalators, cars, golf carts and numerous labor-saving devices is enough to tell the body that it does not need to be very fit. The heart responds accordingly.

Here are just a few case studies which show how useful it

can be to convince the body otherwise; that you do need to stay fit.

A woman once sought a psychologist's help for seemingly incurable depression which had persisted over some years. The prescribed therapy was running. After only two weeks, her depression had lifted and only returned when an injury kept her off the road for three weeks. When she resumed, the depression again was banished.

Two psychologists once put a group of unfit university students through a physical training course three times a week for six weeks. By the programme's end, those who had depression problems at the start had cheered up considerably.

A very inactive office-worker once took an ergometer test and was truly astounded to discover how unfit he had become. But he should not have been surprised. He was desk-bound all day, would never walk anywhere if he could ride and most nights rested in a comfortable armchair in front of a television set. Immediately upon starting an exercise programme a very profound mental change took place. Not only did he feel much better but his outlook upon life and the world brightened and his vague feelings of tension and anxiety largely disappeared.

Two university professors once decided that their out-of-condition, office-bound colleagues needed an exercise programme. After some weeks of it, they were surprised to find that not only were their charges more relaxed but had greater self-confidence, more extraversion and seemed more stable. These traits are typically those of professional athletes, who are usually more adventurous and self-assured than the average.

Why does exercise have such beneficial effects? Why may it reduce anxiety and depression? There are several schools of thought.

One view, held by some exercise physiologists, is that exercise directly reduces tension. Physical tension leads to mental tension and if you get those tense muscles to work out, they can only relax afterward. Because of the direct mind-body connection here, mental relaxation follows.

A second view is that exercise eases depression because it gives a sense of mastery, a sense of efficacy. As we saw in Chapter 6, we all need to believe that we can affect the world at times. Depression can result from the opposite feeling, that the great immovable outside world cannot be altered one little bit, that we are doomed to be swept along with its powerful and irresistible currents. Succeeding at an exercise programme can help counteract that feeling. You set out to complete your daily exercise programme and you did it; you succeeded. You ran those three miles and did those fifty sit-ups. You are helping to keep the only body you have in good shape and health. So doing well at your programme encourages the belief that you can succeed at other things too.

Depression and anxiety may also be eased because of the release of certain chemicals in the brain. Recent research has shown that the brain has its own indigenous "opiates", which are released to deaden pain. This may occur during prolonged exercise, and have a similar effect to a shot of actual opiates, at least for a while.

How much exercise do you need? Not really a great deal. Exercise physiologists believe that maintaining a sustained heart rate for about twenty minutes per session three times a week may be enough. Running, swimming or bicycle riding are ideal exercises. After only six to eight weeks of such a programme you should be in good shape. Take note of the usual warnings, though. See your doctor for advice if you are much over thirty or have a history of heart complaints. Begin to exercise slowly and slowly increase the amount you perform. If you have been sedentary for a long time, you need to very gradually get back to fitness. Many books and courses are available that set out a programme for individual needs.

CHAPTER 8

Relaxation and Anxiety-management Techniques

Here we look at some ways to acquire one of the most important coping skills of all; the ability to relax, to control anxiety. Over the last few decades, psychologists have come up with a set of methods to help even the most tense person remain calm. The power to relax greatly aids coping for several reasons. First, it can be used purely as a palliative, a calming agent for situations where there really is nothing productive to be done. Second, it should enable one to act more effectively in stress-inducing situations. As we saw in Chapter 1, performance deteriorates at higher levels of anxiety, at the upper reaches of the Yerkes–Dodson curve. Thus even someone who knows what to do in a given situation may be prevented from doing it because of too-great arousal.

Third, being too anxious can prevent a person learning, when necessary, more effective ways of behaving in certain circumstances. One example is the kind of social-skill deficits covered in Chapter 5. If such a deficit means much anxiety for a person in certain social situations, that strong internal signal may absorb much of his or her attention. Rather than looking outwards, for signals and feedback from others, concentrating on choosing words carefully and experimenting with new ways of behaving, a person may just look inwards.

We look first at some general methods of relaxation, ways to attack anxiety from a variety of sources. These methods can be applied to numerous daily hassles; to stay cool when getting into a dispute with a neighbor or landlord, when dating, or for a young mother who faces a trying day with the children. Then we look at some ways of battling anxiety that arises from specific sources. These include mild phobias, as of dogs, snakes or flying, and recurring stress-inducing thoughts.

RELAXATION TECHNIQUES

The last ten years have seen the popularization of many different relaxation methods. They range from yoga, massage, hypnosis, and biofeedback to the techniques covered here. All methods have four factors in common which promote relaxation, according to noted cardiologist Herbert Benson. First, they take place in a quiet environment, somewhere free of stress-inducing distractions. Second, the relaxer adopts a comfortable position. Third, he or she has something to focus attention on, be it a specific tension source, a single word in the case of transcendental meditation, or the hypnotist's watch or voice. Finally, the relaxer has a passive mental attitude, one that blocks out all but that upon which he or she focuses.

PROGRESSIVE RELAXATION TRAINING This ubiquitous and highly useful technique goes right back to the 1930s. A physician named Edmund Jacobsen devised and wrote about it. Unfortunately, the world was not quite ready at the time and his ideas slumbered until rediscovered in the 1950s.

Jacobsen reasoned that tension is as much a physical state as a mental one. We feel tension in particular spots, in certain specific muscle groups. Individuals differ in respect to exactly which ones. Some, for instance, may feel it in the legs, others mostly in the neck or the arms, others the forehead. The basic idea behind the technique is to learn to localize exactly where you feel it and then learn to relax those specific muscle groups. And once you are physically relaxed, this state should translate into a mental calm.

Now to the details. To begin, find somewhere peaceful and quiet, free of distractions. Sit comfortably and close your eyes. Then, begin with your toe muscles: clench and then relax them. Just work on the toes alone at first. Tense for about five seconds, relax for about ten. Do this ten times. Then move up to the next muscle group in your body; your foot muscles. Repeat the tensing/relaxing cycle. Gradually work up your body, repeating the cycle with each muscle group in turn, until you reach the top of your head. Move on to the next muscle group, however, only when the one before it is totally relaxed. Try not to work on more than one muscle group at a time; that step comes a bit later. Try the whole workout about once a day for a couple of weeks, just concentrating on the pleasantness of the resulting relaxation feelings.

The next step is to combine the single muscle groups into larger ones. Again, you do this progressively. You might start by combining your toe, foot and ankle muscles into one. Alternately tense and relax this whole group. Then again move to the next combined group, which might be the rest of the leg for example. Keep combining the groups into larger ones until your body is one single unit — one group that you can tense or relax as one.

But, there are a couple of things to avoid. First, do not try to rush. Stick to one session a day and spread the whole procedure out over a few weeks. Second, do not try to compete with yourself (or anyone else). The best approach is a calm, determined and patient one.

CUE-CONTROLLED RELAXATION Next in the bag of methods is cue-controlled relaxation. Here you establish a word or thought as a cue for relaxation. The parallel to the theatre is no accident. An actor's cue tells him when to get out on stage or reel off his next line, while yours tells your body to relax.

To start, again find somewhere comfortable free of distractions. Then try to go into a state of deep relaxation either by the Jacobsen method just described or by another method. For example, you might imagine yourself floating on a peaceful ocean, or high above in the clouds. Or, imagine yourself sinking deeper and deeper into your chair or couch.

Next, pick a target word which for you conjures up some images of tranquillity, for example "calm", "peace", or "relax". Then, for some time just concentrate on your breathing. Focus your whole attention on each breath, slowly inhaling and exhaling. Clear your mind of anything else. Then, as you exhale, think your cue word. Repeat this a number of times, making sure you relax as you do so. Practice this pairing at least fifteen or twenty times for the first session. Repeat the session once a day for several weeks.

What should happen is this. When you exhale, you automatically relax, because letting the breath out is itself a kind of tension release. So, by repeatedly associating this exhalation with a word, you are establishing that word as a cue. And you can use this cue as a relaxer when you need it, again as a coping method.

One final note. Even when your word is well-established as a cue, you may need occasional booster sessions to keep it as one. So, every now and again repeat the entire fifteen to twenty pairing cycles just as in the first session.

AUTOGENIC TRAINING This is a kind of self-hypnosis. The method was developed by two German physicians, Johannes Schultz and Wolfgang Luther, in the 1920s. They applied it to a variety of problems such as general tension and high blood pressure.

To begin, again find somewhere distraction-free. You then need to practise some self-observation. Just watch yourself relax rather than try to actively promote it. First tell yourself that your right arm is heavy, very heavy, so heavy that it is sinking through the floor. Then move to your left arm, your right leg and left leg, repeating the process when each in turn does feel heavy. Following this procedure, say to yourself, "my right arm is heavy and *warm*". Then do this again with the other three limbs as well. Then move to your heart-beat, saying to yourself, "my heart-beat is regular and calm". Then focus on your breathing, keeping it deep and slow, just observing it. Then shift attention to your solar plexus, feeling warmth in it. Finally, feel coolness in your forehead.

The procedure might take months and much practice to master. You should set aside two daily practice sessions of ten or fifteen minutes. Go through the whole routine slowly, only moving to the next step when you have mastered the one before it.

ATTACKING SPECIFIC ANXIETY SOURCES

The above methods are intended to make one generally more relaxed. Often, though, a person may have difficulty only in a single or a few situations. A person might find stressful such situations as public speaking, certain social situations, dealing with superiors, or driving. At the extreme here are phobias, intense anxiety reactions to certain objects. It used to be fashionable to name them, but seems not to be any more. Thus we had zoophobia (fear of animals), agoraphobia (fear of leaving the home) and xenophobia (fear of strangers). These are but a few on a long list.

Phobias and less intense anxiety responses can be picked up in several different ways. The first is the most obvious: by a direct bad experience. One can acquire a fear of dogs after a painful canine bite or one of public speaking after a talk in which one was very nervous, badly prepared and stuttered. A second way is from observing the fear of others: this can somehow rub off. In the London blitz of World War II, for example, children were much more likely to be afraid of the bombing if their parents were. A third way is simply by being told that something is evil and malevolent. Many parents fill their children with fears in this way; of trolls, the devil, other races, and ideologies like Communism. A fourth way is more complex. Sometimes an apparent surface fear can reflect some seemingly unrelated inner conflict. When this is resolved, the fear disappears. An example of this phenomenon is given later in the chapter.

The first two methods covered here for dealing with situational anxiety are systematic desensitization and flooding. But before describing them and how they are best used, it is very helpful to have some notion of why they work. Both are based on a couple of important psychological principles, principles first laid down by a scientist whose name is almost a household word but whose work most people know of only vaguely.

Back in the early part of this century a Russian physiologist named Ivan Pavlov set the stage for much of modern psychology with some interesting experiments on dogs. He was initially interested in digestion (he actually won a Nobel Prize in 1904 for his work on this process) and was studying the early stages of it, salivation. Pavlov had some dogs rigged up in an apparatus such that he could shoot food powder into their mouths and then count the number of drops of saliva they produced as a result. He thus began with a simple reflex, where a stimulus (food) produced the response of salivation. Humans also have this same salivation reflex and lots of other inborn ones as well. A very familiar one is the knee jerk. If someone hits you in the right spot on the knee, your knee will jump up. Another common one is the startle reflex. If you sneak up on someone unawares and suddenly let out a great yell, his or her shoulders will rise, neck go forward and face take on a most characteristic expression. And fear and anxiety are reflexive reactions to some stimuli.

Returning to early twentieth-century Russia; Pavlov noticed something unexpected and interesting. After a dog had been studied for some time, the scientist saw that as soon as he walked into a room where the beast was harnessed, the animal would begin to salivate. Pavlov himself was almost as good as actual food powder in getting the dog to salivate. He had the reflex without the stimulus itself. What was happening? What Pavlov later called *classical conditioning* was taking place. It is a very simple form of learning in which the animal learns to associate two stimuli. In this case, the dogs learned to associate food with the arrival of Pavlov, since the latter usually preceded the former.

The great man then began a research programme to study this conditioning in detail. Rather than using just himself as a stimulus, he trained dogs to salivate to a host of other ones, such as bells, buzzers and lights. Pavlov also studied two other interesting aspects of the phenomenon that are of direct interest to us here. One he called *extinction*. He simply asked what would happen if he stopped pairing the conditioned stimulus with food. For example, an experiment is done in which a buzzer is repeatedly paired with food until the dog salivates to the buzzer itself. What would happen then if he just kept on sounding the buzzer by itself, without giving any more food? The answer is that the response extinguishes, like a candle flame does. Eventually the buzzer ceases to induce salivation. So Pavlov realized that this is a good way of getting rid of an unwanted response to a stimulus — just stop pairing it with the unconditioned stimulus. Is there any other way? Yes, there is *counterconditioning*. This is a procedure which replaces one conditioned response with another. It is sort of a combination of extinction and reconditioning of another response. For example, let us say that we have a dog that salivates to the sound of a bell, because beforehand we have conditioned it to do so. We then try to replace the salivation response by another response, one that is incompatible with salivation and will inhibit it. Thus we could stop pairing the bell with food and instead pair it with electric shock. We would not have a happy animal but we might have one that responded with fear rather than salivation to the bell. Thus we would have counter-conditioned salivation.

This classical conditioning is important in humans because many psychologists believe that we learn a lot of emotional responses in this way. For example, one might develop a healthy fear of snakes after being bitten by one, because the sight of snakes is paired with pain, or a more positive attitude to a political party if it gives out free beer at its rallies. These can be seen as examples of classical conditioning.

With a little theory behind us, we can now look at systematic desensitization and flooding in detail.

SYSTEMATIC DESENSITIZATION This very handy method was devised by psychiatrist Joseph Wolpe in the 1950s for use in treating negative reactions to highly specific stimuli. Here we focus on it as a method to deal with anxiety but it has been successfully used to counter feelings such as anger and jealousy as well. The method is the same regardless of the emotion.

The basic principle involved seems to be counterconditioning, although this is still being debated. The notion is that a person has somewhere in the past learned a particular reaction to a specific class of stimuli that he or she wishes to be rid of. It might be fear of dogs, hatred of people over a certain height, anxiety when having to speak in public, and so on. It is not so important how a person came to react in this particular way.

To begin with you build a hierarchy. A hierarchy is a list of ten to fifteen graded items, arranged in order, each of which gets progressively closer to the stimulus that causes anxiety (or whatever). For example, let us say you wish to expunge a mild dread of public speaking. (This is, incidentally, the worst fear of many people. Surveys often find that people fear public speaking more than war or cancer.) So, a hierarchy might consist of the following items. The first might be a very mild situation that causes very little anxiety; say having a casual conversation with two others. The next step might be talking to three or four

Table 3

Two examples of hierarchies. The first was used with a forty-year-old male who developed a fear of heights; the second with a female student who had a severe examination phobia. Both are adapted from Rimm and Masters (1979).

Height fear

---

1. You are beginning to climb a ladder leaning against the side of your house. You plan to work on the roof. Your hands are on the ladder and your foot is on the first rung.
2. You are halfway up the ladder and you happen to look down. You see the lawn below you and a walkway.
3. Driving with the family, road begins to climb.
4. Driving with family on a coastal highway, with dropoff to the right.
5. On a seashore cliff, approximately 10 metres (30 feet) from edge.
6. On a seashore cliff, approximately 2 metres (6 feet) from edge.
7. Driving with family, approaching mountain summit.
8. In commercial airliner, at time of takeoff.
9. In commercial airliner, at an altitude of 9000 metres (30,000 feet).
10. In airliner, at an altitude of 9000 metres (30,000 feet) with considerable turbulence.
11. On a seaside cliff, approximately half a metre (2 feet) from the edge looking down.
12. Climbing the town water tower to assist in painting, about 3 metres (10 feet) from ground.
13. Same as above, but about 6 metres (20 feet) from ground.
14. On the catwalk around the water tank, painting the tank.

Examination fear

---

1. Four days before an examination.
2. Three days before an examination.
3. Two days before an examination.
4. One day before an examination.
5. The night before an examination.
6. Before the unopened doors of the examination room.
7. Awaiting the distribution of examination papers.
8. The examination paper lies before you.
9. In the process of answering an examination paper.

people, also in an informal setting, then perhaps speaking to half a dozen more formally. Your final item might be the most extreme, the worst that could happen to you when giving a speech. For example, you could be talking to five hundred bored-looking people, most of whom look like they would much rather be somewhere else. A few near the front are whispering to each other, others near the back are chuckling, many seem to be asleep, and a couple are actually drifting out the door. Table 3 gives two examples of hierarchies. Writing a hierarchy may be a bit painful, especially if you put yourself into the situations as you write. If you can, enlist someone's aid or try to completely detach yourself from each situation while you write.

Once you have a hierarchy the next stage is to work through it. Find a quiet place, get comfortable and then relax completely, using one of the techniques mentioned in the last section. Then, imagine the first item in your hierarchy. Put yourself right into the scene that you have depicted, keeping yourself relaxed. If you feel any anxiety, you may need to put in a less severe first step to your hierarchy. When you are totally relaxed in response to the stimuli in the scene, move up to the next step in your hierarchy and keep relaxed to that. Then progressively move up until eventually you reach the last and most anxiety-provoking item. Only move to the next item when you can feel totally relaxed with the preceding one. If a particular item does cause too much anxiety, move back to the one before it and relax again. Another thing to try to avoid is blotting out part of the scene in each item. Quite a few people do this to try to reduce anxiety; but guard against it. Put yourself into the entire situation. Visualize everything vividly.

You should not try to go through the entire hierarchy in one session, or even five sessions. A very common mistake is to try to rush things. Take it slowly. Have no more than one session a day, which should never last more than about twenty minutes. Begin each session with the last item in your hierarchy that you were able to successfully relax to.

Do not try real-life contact with the stimuli that cause you anxiety until you have successfully gone right through the hierarchy. Then only do so in small doses, trying to keep relaxed throughout.

Systematic desensitization is a very useful technique. It has been successfully applied to a variety of fears and other problematic reactions. They range from anger when driving, asthma, stuttering, fear of animals, of childbirth, to racial anger.

Two more important points need to be mentioned here, ones to be aware of when using this method. The first is that many fears reflect some skill deficit. For example, someone may be afraid of public speaking because he or she does not prepare well enough, and has not learned adequate speaking skills. In such a context, the fear is quite adaptive in a sense because it may protect the person from harm. Rimm and Masters (1979) told of a quite amusing case along these lines. A man turned up at a psychologist's office asking to be desensitized from his fears of brawls in seedy bars in San Francisco. He spent much time in such bars and wanted to lose his fear of brawls so that "he could beat everyone up". The psychologist pointed out that his small size and lack of fighting ability would mean that he could not hope to stay desensitized for long. A couple of fights would rekindle his fear very quickly. Thus sometimes one may need to do some specific training in a skill and at other times simply need to recognize that a certain fear is quite adaptive.

The second point is one mentioned earlier; a particular surface fear may reflect complex psychodynamics. The thinking behind it may be mostly unconscious and hard to get at. Arnold Lazarus tells of a man complaining of a bridge phobia, he being afraid to cross the Bay Bridge from San Francisco to Oakland. Desensitization had not helped eliminate it. As it turned out, his real fear was of taking on more responsibility at work. The bridge phobia prevented him taking on a job with greater responsibility for which he would have needed to cross the bridge every day.

FLOODING   This is a rather extreme measure, not at all a good idea for the sensitive. The basic idea is to face the source of anxiety (or anger or jealousy) at its worst, in imagination. There are no intermediate steps to it as in systematic desensitization; instead you leap in at the deep end. So, your anxiety level reaches a peak, you experience the reaction at its worst. Inhibition may then build up, either through extinction or counterconditioning, and the reaction may subsequently lessen. Parents sometimes use a variant of it when they toss a child into the deep end of a swimming pool.

For example, say one wishes to expunge a fear of snakes. Imagine yourself in a pit full of cobras and pythons for a time. If it is the dark, imagine yourself lost in a forest on a moonless, stormy night. If it is public speaking, imagine yourself out on stage in front of ten-thousand people. Once the fear is confronted at its worst, it may be inhibited to some extent.

A variation on the technique, to make it even more potent, is to visualize the most horrible consequences possible in the feared situation. For example, with a spider phobia, one might see oneself as caught in a huge web, with an enormous spider heading for you. Or, see yourself trapped in the pit with many different types of snake crawling all over you. (Again, this method is not for the sensitive.)

Flooding has been recently used successfully to treat Vietnam veterans. As mentioned in Chapter 4, many have very bad memories of the war and what they had to do when fighting in it. They are often placed in a chair and asked to relive some of their worst experiences in imagination. This is done repeatedly for several sessions.

ANXIETY MANAGEMENT TRAINING (AMT) AMT was devised by Suinn and Richardson (1971) as a useful alternative to systematic desensitization. Sometimes the latter can take much time to use, and the hierarchies a lot of creative thought and effort to write. And that method usually does not give one the power to deal with fears other than those on the hierarchy actually worked through. AMT seems to have a somewhat more general effect.

The idea at its heart is to use the presence of anxiety, that inner feeling of tension and unease, as a cue. Use it as a cue that tells you to bring to bear one of several techniques to try to banish the feeling altogether. You learn to recognize the onset of anxiety, so as to be able to bring immediate control methods to bear on it.

Now for the details. First pick a couple of scenes that you can easily visualize. One should be anxiety-arousing, but not one that produces an overwhelming fear. It could be an image from a horror movie, a vision of yourself about to speak to a large crowd, a lion about to pounce; something of that sort. The second scene should be one that you find relaxing and peaceful, one that produces the opposite reaction. It could be an image of you on a picnic on a lazy, sunny afternoon, soaking up sun on the beach, or blissfully savoring the sensations of a hot tub.

Now to the training part. Sit comfortably somewhere reasonably free of distractions. Then visualize the anxiety-provoking scene — put yourself into it until you feel at least some mild anxiety. Then quickly terminate the scene and replace it with your relaxation scene, taking care to relax as you do. Practise this alternation of images for a number of trials, until you get adept at terminating the anxiety scene and the mild unease that goes along with it. Then later try some different anxiety-inducing and relaxation-inducing images, especially if you start to habituate to the first two, that is they begin to elicit less of a response. Once you have mastered this part, which may take several hours of training, you are ready for the last phase. Here you need to pick some real anxiety-provoking stimuli, not just imaginary ones. It could be a tape-recording of readings from Edgar Allan Poe, some dark and gloomy mood music, or some phobic object. For example, if you fear snakes, use a model or even a real one. Again apply your management technique to the anxiety. Practise blocking out the negative sensations produced by the actual object by switching to your scenes of relaxation. Make a real effort to focus on your pleasant images. You may thus find that the anxiety becomes more manageable. And finally, imagine yourself successfully coping with anxiety in a scene when not actually in contact with the feared object. That exercise may help enhance feelings of self-efficacy.

Just one more point to mention. First, nip the stress reaction in the bud, so to speak. It is important to catch the stress response in its early stages and start coping then. A full-blown attack is much more difficult to control.

AMT seems to work quite well with many people. Suinn and Richardson themselves tried it out on a group of students suffering from mathematics anxiety. The latter is a freezing up (and sometimes even a panic reaction) upon exposure to algebra, a morbid dread of geometry, a crippling fear of calculus! Many of the previously afflicted young victims had considerably reduced their anxiety levels after some training, enough at least to actually start learning some maths.

CONTROLLING ANXIETY-INDUCING THOUGHTS Many of us at some time are bothered by recurring, unwanted thoughts.

They can include continually reliving some social blunder, over-concern with a mistake on the job, or guilt over some past misdeed. Others can be continually thinking about some recent loss, or how events might have gone if one had done something different. At the extreme of this spectrum are obsessions, common in people with obsessive-compulsive neurosis.

Normally, we are freed from most such thoughts by habituation, by working through them, or by using some defence mechanism. But these may go awry, for any of a variety of reasons. When this happens, one or both of the following techniques may help control such stress-inducing thoughts.

The first method is an active attempt to habituate to them. The simple idea is to repeatedly expose yourself to them, continually think them, preferably in a state of relaxation, and see if they lose their potency. Parkinson and Rachman (1980) carried out a study which suggested this may indeed work. One can either try long periods of four or five minutes where you continually go over troublesome thoughts or a series of two-minute trials interspersed with a minute or two of relaxation with a blank state of mind. Again, it may take a number of trials to become habituated, with booster sessions to stay that way.

Another method is thought-stopping. To use it you first need some training sessions somewhere quiet where you can yell. To begin, when you feel such an unwanted thought coming on, at the top of your voice shout "STOP". The thought should dis-appear, as your full attention is taken up by your voice. If the thought comes back, repeat the process. Train yourself to think "STOP" (with an exclamation mark) so that you can use it when unable to actually yell, as in a theatre or library. It is also useful to try to associate pleasant thoughts or experiences with the word "stop" or whatever other one you use. Those pleasant images then take the place of the anxiety-laden ones.

CHAPTER 9

Stress Inoculation Training

Medicine was revolutionized many decades ago by the discovery of inoculation. This elegant idea has since saved countless lives. It rests on a simple fact. We all have an immune system to fight off invading hordes of bacteria and viruses which otherwise might produce lethal infections. But many diseases, such as smallpox and typhoid, strike a full-force blow which can overpower an unprepared immune system. The way round this is to give small, weakened doses of each deadly invader (or a similar organism) which the system can learn to recognize and cope with, so that the defences strengthen. If the actual disease organisms do later attack, the altered immune system can more easily fend them off.

In the last decade or so, the same idea has been rigorously applied to managing stress. The analogy is not perfect but is interesting. Stressors are in some ways like micro-organisms in that they attack and we defend. We all have some existing defences against stressors, some ways of coping. But, as has been said, these defences vary greatly in strength from person to person. Some are not strong enough to withstand really hefty doses of stress (and indeed most of us collapse if the stressors are really strong enough). So either they suffer more or try to cope in sometimes maladaptive ways. But sometimes the internal defences against stress can be strengthened just as the immune system can be against microbes, by a series of weak, small doses. One can learn to deal with them without being overwhelmed and continued practice at handling minor stressors allows one to better manage the big ones when they hit.

The stress inoculation notion has been used for centuries in child-rearing, in certain schools and in military academies. In the latter, first-year cadets are frequently given a very hard time by their upper-class fellows. They get much verbal and sometimes physical abuse, and are given difficult, meaningless tasks to do.

One point of this no doubt is to weed out the really unfit, those who cannot learn to take it. Presumably they are seen as likely to make poor officers. But the main idea is that all this flak will help to strengthen the survivors' capacity to deal with the rigors of later command and combat.

On might ask here the following question. When are such stressful experiences inoculators and when are they simply traumas, leading to syndromes described in Chapter 4? To pose this question another way, when is an event a crisis that leads to growth and when is it a trauma that leads to long-term harm? Benner, Roskies and Lazarus (1980) suggest one possibility. If a person can either acquire or draw on resources to cope effectively, the stressor is likely to be a strengthener. But if he or she is unable to do so and gets overwhelmed, it is likely to be a trauma.

The stress inoculation idea was developed into an explicit training programme by Novaco (1975), Donald Meichenbaum (1977), Turk (1978) and some others. I describe this progamme in some detail and some problems that may arise in learning it. It has been tested with a variety of different groups and stressors and seems to work quite well. It aids in managing anxiety, has helped groups like policemen better handle provocation arising from their job, and it helps in managing the stress of chronic pain. One convincing example of its usefulness was in a study by Langer, Janis and Wolper (1975). They trained a group of patients about to go through the nerve-racking experience of major surgery. Their nurses reported that these patients as a result seemed to be much more relaxed and tranquil, much more prepared for the operation than patients not given the programme. They also needed fewer analgesic and sedative drugs afterwards.

The programme has three phases. Training in two of them overlaps to some extent with what we have covered in earlier chapters. But, to describe the procedure fully, we may need to go over just a bit of old ground.

PHASE 1: AN EDUCATION ABOUT STRESS

The first phase involves learning a way of thinking about the stress reaction and how it can be handled. Stress inoculators promote a particular view of stress and how we respond, one partly based on the research of psychologist Stanley Schachter from the 1960s. This view of stress is not totally free of criticism (few theories are) but it is a useful way to look at stress and its management.

This view sees emotional reactions (fear, anger, disgust, etc.) as having two parts. The first is sheer physiological arousal. The body gets aroused by a fearful object, an anxiety-provoking situation or an anger-provoking one. So the familiar physical symptoms erupt; increased heart rate, faster breathing, tensing of muscles and so on. The second part of the response sees the mind at work, sparked off by these physical signs. It starts interpreting them, attributing the arousal to various things, and labelling the arousal as an emotion. Numerous thoughts, images, and what are referred to as self-statements occur; feelings of helplessness, catastrophizing thoughts, and so on. We are likely to start an internal dialogue, which in an anxiety-inducing situation might include statements such as, "Oh, this situation is really terrible. I just cannot face it. I feel just terrible." Or "I am about to give up, this is beyond my capacity to cope." Such thinking may push one's arousal level up even further. For example, statements about your perceived inadequacy or images of you faltering and going under in a public-speaking situation may be disruptive. As we see in the next section, this conceptualization of the stress reaction leads to some sound thoughts about ways to handle it.

This view also sees the stress experience and a person's coping with it not as a full-blown, overwhelming panic reaction but as having four distinct stages. The first stage is before the stressor has arrived, where you are actively preparing for it. You collect all the information you can about what you will face, make a plan on how to cope, decide which coping techniques are best to use, and get ready to use them. This can all happen in a few minutes, hours or days before the stress storm; the minutes before giving a speech or making a date, before asking the boss for a raise or confronting a subordinate over his misbehavior, going to court or parachuting from a plane. The second stage consists of seeing yourself as possibly being temporarily over-whelmed by the stressor, at least in its first few moments. The third sees you confronting the stressor and handling it, using one

124

or more of the many coping techniques. In the final stage, you reward yourself for successfully coping. The principles in these stages will become clearer in the next couple of sections where the techniques in each are described in detail.

PHASE 2: COPING SKILLS TRAINING

Now begins the active training in more coping skills. Here one learns some new ways to fight the small doses of stress to be encountered in Phase 3, and thus to better battle the hefty real-life ones. This section is a new menu of techniques. Pick out the ones that best suit your personal style, and use them along with others from previous chapters. The relaxation methods of Chapter 8, for example, can be used here as well. Also, it is important to be flexible. Try a technique and replace it with another if results are not satisfactory. Also vary methods across situations and stressors. For example, for you methods 1 and 2 may be very useful for stressor A but not for B. Stressor B may be best handled by methods 3 and 4. Your best methods for particular stressors should become clear with practice and experience.

DISTRACTION METHODS   Imagine that you are at a cocktail party, having a lively talk with someone interesting. A buzz of conversations and other sounds are going on all around at the same time. Some other guests are conversing loudly, others are deeply immersed in a party game, and a stereo is blaring as well. Yet somehow you do not seem to notice all this babble. The noises are apparently blocked out as your attention stays focused on the words and actions of your partner. You concentrate on just what you want to and eliminate all the distractions. The same thing happens while watching a good movie at a theatre. Again, many distractions occur all around; people chatting, moving about, and munching popcorn. But your attention seems wholly taken up by the action on the silver screen and you block them all out.

These situations illustrate a very important feature of the human mind: it can only really focus on one thing at a time. Countless experiments have shown this limit again and again. People cannot concentrate fully on even two different streams of information coming in; only one can be fully comprehended. As at the cocktail party, though, we can largely decide what we want to concentrate on, what stream we wish to pay attention to. Psychologists often make an analogy to a television set. A set can only be tuned to one channel. The other channels might as well not be there. However, as with a television, we can voluntary change channels, decide what stream we want to focus on.

This limit to the human mind can be put to great use in coping with stressors, particularly ones like chronic or acute pain, annoyances like a barking neighborhood dog, hammering from a construction site next door, or internal reactions to stress such as anxiety and anger. The principle is very simple. Such stressors (or reactions) can be seen as streams of information. So, rather than focus on them and suffer, shift your attention to a different stream and thus block them out. Or, keep focused on them but use your imagination to convert them into a non-stressful stream. If you necessarily shift to something else, you may barely notice the stressor.

Now to the details. The first technique using this principle has the appropriate name of *attention–diversion*. You simply pick and focus on a stream of information incompatible with the one you wish to be rid of. For example, if trying to divert away a headache or backache, you might do numerous problems in mental arithmetic, count all the cracks in the ceiling or count all the windows in each house along your street. Or, just concentrate on a particular sensation in your body, one that is different from the source of pain or the feeling of anxiety. For example, imagine your left big toe tingling and stay focused on that sensation.

I use this simple method during exercise. Toward the end of a long run or after many lengths of the local swimming pool, my body starts to hurt and tells me to stop this foolish workout. I also get thoughts like "why am I doing so much exercise, I don't really need to be so fit", and so on. This is always a critical time and I do my best to divert attention both from the pain and the resulting thoughts and apparent good reasons for stopping. I think deeply about some work problem or about some fundamental scientific principle and all its ramifications. Sometimes I imagine that I am running across a dark moor with numerous ferocious hounds in hot pursuit. This technique usually blots out the pain signals for long enough to let me finish.

Meichenbaum (1977) gives two interesting examples

of its use from the past. The philosopher Immanuel Kant suffered from the painful disease gout, which he sometimes coped with by concentrating on a name and its many associations. This would, he reported, distract his attention and dull the pain enough to allow him to sleep.

During an unsavory period of history — the Inquisition — with its tortures and executions, some victims spontaneously used this technique.

Some rascals trusted so strongly in the secrets they possessed to make themselves insensible to pain, that they voluntarily gave themselves up as prisoners, to cleanse themselves of certain sins. Some use certain words pronounced in a low voice and others writings, which they hide on some part of their body. The first one I recognized as using some sort of charm, surprised us by his more than natural firmness, because after the first stretching of the rack, he seemed to sleep as quietly as if he had been in a good bed, without lamenting, complaining or crying, and when the stretching was repeated two or three times, he still remained as motionless as a statue. This made us suspect that he was provided with some charm, and to resolve the doubt he was stripped as naked as his hand. Yet after a careful search nothing was found on him but a little piece of paper on which were the figures of the three kings, with these words on the other side: "Beautiful star which delivered the Magi from Herod's persecution, deliver me from all torment." This paper was stuffed in his left ear. Now although the paper had been taken away from him he still appeared insensible to the torture, because when it applied he muttered words between his teeth which we could not hear, and as he persevered in his denials, it was necessary to send him back to prison. [Cited by Bernheim, 1964.]

The next set of techniques is based on the same principle but makes use of fantasy, of imagination, for the distraction. One uses imagery to transform the pain or stress sensations into something else and thus short-circuit their path to consciousness. Fantasy can be so used in several ways. First, one can construct a fantasy, a scene that is totally incompatible with your present experience. For example, if you are stuck with a severe backache, great tension or have been seething with anger for days over someone's misdeed, instead imagine yourself lying on the beach on a sunny day. Or, visualize yourself at a rock concert or the opera hearing your favorite piece of music. Feel yourself floating on the ocean or up among the clouds, free of all sensations except relaxation and peace. Or concentrate on a feather floating down from a great height. Put yourself right into each scene and concentrate on the sensations and visions in it.

Another method is to change the context in which pain or some negative feeling occurs. For example, say you have a sore arm. Imagine yourself as a spy or fleeing criminal just shot in the arm. Construct a story, a fantasy around this. You can even acknowledge the negative feelings but use imagination to transform them into something else, or dismiss them as trivial. Imagine a sore back as shot up with novocaine, and therefore completely numb. Tell yourself you are a robot invulnerable to pain and stress. Transform feelings of anger into ones of great strength. The possibilities are limited only by one's powers of imagination.

It is very important to remember, however, that pain is a warning sign that something is wrong. Make sure you first check any out with a doctor, before simply trying to divert them away.

Such a constructive use of fantasy can relieve many kinds of stressors. Many people spontaneously use it to survive boring, repetitive and otherwise soul-destroying situations that stay the same day after day. One summer I spent in a factory next to a convict working on a day-release programme. We put in a fifty-five-hour week, always doing pretty much the same task. I once asked him how he had stood it so long and how he seemed to coast so easily through each day. His answer: "I am never really here; I am always off somewhere else, thinking about what I have done, what I am going to do." We saw the same phenomenon among prisoners of war in Chapter 4. A famous writer also reported that he survived years of prison in a similar way, by conjuring up in imagination vast cathedrals and palaces and journeying through them. A more formal study once put some university students through a dull session pressing a button whenever a light happened to flash, which was not often. Talks with the students afterward revealed that the ones who got through the task readily and pleasantly had put their imaginations to work making it interesting. They were not subjects in a boring experiment, they were radar operators watching for an enemy attack warned of by the light. They were sprinters anxiously awaiting the signal to start running. They made the situation a game or a challenge. Such use of imagination to counter negative physical feelings was well summed up in an oft-quoted remark by Satchel Paige: "If your stomach disputes you lie down and pacify it with cool thoughts".

SELF-INSTRUCTIONAL TRAINING   The other aspect of stress-inoculation training involves changing what you say to yourself. We saw earlier in this chapter that the stress reaction is often accompanied by many self-statements. These seem automatic and can intensify the emotional impact of the experience. We start this talking to ourselves early in life. In part, early self-talk helps direct our behavior and thus aids us in learning new skills. The Soviet psychologist Alexander Luria proposed that children learn to carry out and inhibit many actions in three distinct phases. First, the talk of others (usually adults) directs the child, "Now hold the bat like this Jimmy and swing . . .", "Sally, first you thread this shoelace over this one like so . . .", and so on. In the second phase, the child's own speech takes the place of the adult's. The words are much the same but the child says them instead of the adult. In the final phase, the child's own speech guides the actions. Here is an amusing illustration of the final phase from a three-and-a-half-year-old child playing alone:

The wheels go here, the wheels go here. Oh, we need to start it all over again. We have to close it up. See, it closes up. We're starting all over again. Do you know why we wanted to do that? Because I needed it to go a different way. Isn't it pretty clever, don't you think? But we have to cover up the motor just like a real car. [From Kohlberg, Yaeger and Hjertholm, 1968.]

One of the most obvious cases in which adults use self-talk is in learning a new skill, such as typing, swinging a golf club or operating a computer terminal. We begin with a set of verbal orders, and follow them. With time the words drop out, and eventually the task is automatic, without needing any thought to be carried out. Learning to drive a car is a good example. At first you memorize numerous statements about what to do; how to coordinate the clutch and gears, how and when to operate the brakes, and so on. For a long time the movements and their co-ordination are jerky, poor, and subject to much self-direction. But with time, the self-statements drop out, the whole performance becomes very smooth and you can drive with little attention devoted to what you are doing. It then is possible to carry on a conversation or listen to music at the same time. When the task is done automatically, self-talk can actually be harmful.

During a stress reaction, as mentioned, such self-statements tend to occur and can make the situation worse. Here are a couple more examples to drive the point home. Consider a person with a strong fear of public-speaking just mounting the podium to address a large group. His arousal level is high and sparks off numerous self-statements, "Boy, am I nervous. I can really feel the tension. With all this anxiety, there is no way I can get this speech off smoothly. I know I am going to crack up. Look, a few people are walking out already. They know how bad I will be. I wish this were over." A girl out on her first driving lesson might have thoughts along the same lines, "Oh, this is horrible, it is so dangerous out here. I cannot handle this situation, I am going to make a horrible mistake and have an accident."

These statements have the effect of partly guiding behavior and partly making the situation worse, because they are negative. The counter to this problem, the way to defeat this self-fulfilling prophecy, is a two-pronged attack on the self-talk. The first prong is simply to be aware of one's negative self-statements during a stressful experience. Monitor them, recognize their essential irrationality, and realize how much they contribute to the intensity of stress. You can test this out in a mildly stressful situation or in imagination. The next step is to replace the negative statements with positive ones, ones that promote effective coping. Some examples of statements are in Tables 4, 5 and 6. Fortify yourself with a list of these and during a stress reaction repeat them to yourself. It is important to try to do this with conviction. A mechanical, half-hearted dialogue will not help much at all. Convince yourself of their worth, and aggressively repeat them.

For particular situations you may wish to draw up a specific, idiosyncratic list. With time, your use of the self-statements may become automatic and the whole coping performance smooth, just as with driving a car.

Table 4

Examples of coping self-statements rehearsed in stress-inoculation training
(from Meichenbaum, 1974).

Preparing for a stressor

What is it you have to do?

You can develop a plan to deal with it.

Just think about what you can do about it. That's better than
getting anxious.

No negative self-statements: just think rationally.

Don't worry: worry won't help anything.

Maybe what you think is anxiety is eagerness to confront the
stressor.

Confronting and handling a stressor

Just "psych" yourself up — you can meet this challenge.

You can convince yourself to do it. You can reason your fear away.

One step at a time: you can handle the situation.

Don't think about fear; just think about what you have to do.
Stay relevant.

This anxiety is what the doctor said you would feel.

It's a reminder to use your coping exercises.

This tenseness can be an ally; a cue to cope.

Relax; you're in control. Take a slow deep breath.

Ah, good.

Coping with the feeling of being overwhelmed

When fear comes, just pause.

Keep the focus on the present; what is it you have to do?

Label your fear from 0 to 10 and watch it change.

You should expect your fear to rise.

Don't try to eliminate fear totally; just keep it manageable.

Reinforcing self-statements

It worked; you did it.

Wait until you tell your therapist (or group) about this.

It wasn't as bad as you expected.

You made more out of your fear than it was worth.

Your damn ideas — that's the problem. When you control them,
you control your fear.

It's getting better each time you use the procedures.

You can be pleased with the progress you're making.

You did it!

Table 5
More examples of self-statements (from Turk, 1978).

A. Preparing for the intense stimulation before it becomes too strong. Self-instructions and statements that can be made include:
  1 What is it I have to do? (viewing the situation as a problem that you can do something about).
  2 I can develop a plan to deal with it (preparing oneself by making a plan or mental outline of how you will deal with the sensations when they arise).
  3 Just think about what I have to do (focusing on what the situation requires).
  4 Think of the things that I can use to help cope (review all the strategies that you know and that may be helpful).
  5 Don't worry; worrying won't help anything (use any anxiety or worry as a cue to remind you to focus on what you have to do).
  6 Remember, I can shift my attention to anything I want to (reassure yourself about your ability to employ various coping strategies).
  7 When I use mental imagery, I'll see how vivid I can make the scene (review various aspects of the different images and strategies that can be used).

B. Confronting and handling the intense stimulation (self-instructions and statements that can be made at this phase include):
  1 I can meet this challenge (view the situation as a challenge that you deal with).
  2 One step at a time, I can handle the situation (don't do everything at once and don't be overwhelmed; rather, use each of the skills you have learned).
  3 Just relax, breathe deeply, and use one of the strategies (review and use any of the strategies that you have outlined in your plan for coping).
  4 I won't think about any pain, just about what I have to do (focus your attention on the task at hand and what you can do right now to help to cope).
  5 I'm feeling tense: that can be an ally, a cue to switch strategies and to take some slow deep breaths (expect to feel tense at times; that's not unusual, but use your tenseness as a cue to relax and to review which strategy to employ next).
  6 Remember, I can switch back to some strategies that I used before but switched from (there is no reason why you can't return to some strategies already used).

Table 5 (Continued)

C. Coping with thoughts and feelings that arise at critical moments (when you notice that the intensity of the sensations seems to be increasing or you think you can't go on any more). Self-instructions or statements that can be made at this phase include:

1 When I feel pain, just pause, keep focusing on what I have to do.
2 Don't try to eliminate the pain totally, just keep it manageable (remember, you expected to detect some intense stimulation, but don't overreact and make things worse).
3 I knew the sensations would rise; just keep them under control (don't magnify the intensity of the sensations you experience).
4 Remember, there are a lot of things I can do; I can keep things under control (you have been taught a number of different strategies that will help you keep the intense stimulation under control).
5 Things are going pretty bad; I can't take any more — just pause; don't make things worse. I'll review my plan of strategies to see what I switch to (sometimes you may have unpleasant thoughts or feelings; use those as cues to review the strategies available to you).
6 My arm looks terrible; things are falling apart; I better stop — relax. I can focus my attention on something else; keep things under control (if you find yourself focusing on unpleasant sensations or thoughts, remember you can choose what you will focus your attention upon).

D. Self-reflection and positive self-statements. Throughout the three phases outlined above you might evaluate your performance. For example, how am I doing, that worked pretty well, etc. Remember, people frequently criticize themselves but rarely praise their behavior. Throughout a stressful situation evaluate how you are doing. If you think you should be doing better you can use that as a cue to try different strategies. If you are doing well you should give yourself a "pat on the back". Self-reflective statements that might be used throughout a stressful situation:

1 That's it. I've outlined what I have to do, what strategies I can use and which ones I will switch to.
2 I'm doing pretty well; it's not as hard as I thought.
3 I'm doing better at this all the time.
4 I let negative thoughts interfere with using my plan.
5 Wait until I tell the trainer which things worked best.
6 I knew I could handle it; I'm doing pretty well.
7 I'm doing better than I expected; wait until I tell my mother.

Table 6

Examples of self-statements rehearsed in stress-inoculation training for controlling anger (from Novaco, 1975).

Preparing for provocation

This is going to upset me, but I know how to deal with it.

What is it that I have to do?

I can work out a plan to handle this.

I can manage the situations. I know how to regulate my anger.

If I find myself getting upset, I'll know what to do.

There won't be any need for an argument.

Try not to take this too seriously.

This could be a testy situation, but I believe in myself.

Time for a few deep breaths of relaxation. Feel comfortable, relaxed, and at ease.

Easy does it. Remember to keep your sense of humor.

Impact and confrontation

Stay calm. Just continue to relax.

As long as I keep my cool, I'm in control.

Just roll with the punches; don't get bent out of shape.

Think of what you want to get out of this.

You don't need to prove yourself.

There is no point in getting mad.

Don't make more out of this than you have to.

I'm not going to let him get to me.

Look for the positives. Don't assume the worst or jump to conclusions.

It's really a shame that he has to act like this.

For someone to be that irritable, he must be awfully unhappy.

If I start to get mad, I'll just be banging my head against the wall. So I might as well just relax.

There is no need to doubt myself. What he says doesn't matter.

I'm on top of this situation and it's under control.

Coping with arousal

My muscles are starting to feel tight. Time to relax and slow things down.

Getting upset won't help.

It's just not worth it to get so angry.

I'll let him make a fool of himself.

134

Table 6 (Continued)

I have a right to be annoyed, but let's keep the lid on.

Time to take a deep breath.

Let's take the issue point by point.

My anger is a signal of what I need to do.

Time to instruct myself.

I'm not going to get pushed around, but I'm not going haywire either.

Try to reason it out. Treat each other with respect.

Let's try a cooperative approach. Maybe we are both right.

Negatives lead to more negatives. Work constructively.

He'd probably like me to get really angry. Well I'm going to disappoint him.

I can't expect people to act the way I want them to.

Take it easy, don't get pushy.

Reflecting on the provocation

   a. When conflict is unresolved:

     Forget about the aggravation. Thinking about it only makes you upset.

     These are difficult situations, and they take time to straighten out.

     Try to shake it off. Don't let it interfere with your job.

     I'll get better at this as I get more practice.

     Remember relaxation. It's a lot better than anger.

     Can you laugh about it? It's probably not so serious.

     Don't take it personally.

     Take a deep breath.

   b. When conflict is resolved or coping is successful:

     I handled that one pretty well. It worked!

     That wasn't as hard as I thought.

     It could have been a lot worse.

     I could have gotten more upset than it was worth.

     I actually got through that without getting angry.

     My pride can sure get me into trouble, but when I don't take things too seriously, I'm better off.

     I guess I've been getting upset for too long when it wasn't even necessary.

     I'm doing better at this all the time.

Finally, reward yourself for coping well when you have finished. Once again, some good positive self-statements should suffice, such as "I handled that pretty well", "That could have been much worse", "I am getting better at this coping business all the time".

PHASE 3: APPLICATION

Once the above techniques are mastered and the self-statements well-learned, it is time to try them out. So now takes place the actual inoculation. When the preliminaries are done, small doses of stress can be self-administered. Before beginning, however, make sure that you do indeed have some techniques fully down pat. Otherwise failure in this application phase may have a disproportionate effect on feelings of self-efficacy, of belief that you can successfully use them. Also be sure to persevere in this phase. Do not give up easily.

First you need to assemble a set of stress-inducing implements or images and apply them in mild doses. Exercise (provided you are reasonably fit) can be used as a stressor. You could also take in a series of mildly stressful movies, from graphic war pictures and documentaries to horror movies. This phase can also take place in imagination. Draw up a list of stress-inducing situations, be they ones in which you are provoked, embarrassed, or where you fail dismally at some task in front of many people. These situations can be graded, just as in systematic desensitization, and you can work through them progressively in the same way.

Another way to conduct this phase is to actually role-play stress-inducing situations. Probably this is best done with a partner. Take a situation, convince yourself that you are really in it, and act it out. For example, if you wish to better deal with anger (if you are easily provoked) act out a series of progressively more provoking situations. The first could be a mild one, such as a shop clerk deliberately short-changing you a few cents. The final one might be serious verbal abuse from someone. Actually put yourself into the situation, and use the coping techniques to stay cool.

Finally, note just a couple more points. First, to repeat an earlier warning, keep the stress levels quite low and only increase them when you have adequately coped with the previous level. Otherwise you may quite easily be overwhelmed. The second is to use as wide a variety of stressors as you can. Try to avoid just sticking with one that is easy to use. Otherwise your coping skills may not generalize very well; they will stay specific to just one type of stressor and so will not be much use. The last point is to move slowly, making sure that you get a lot of practice. Do not become discouraged if progress is sometimes slow. That is inevitable with learning any skill and will be the case in following the stress-inoculation programme.

CHAPTER 10

Techniques to Counter Faulty Thinking

In Douglas Adams's marvellous *Hitchhiker's Guide to the Galaxy* series is a character called Marvin the paranoid android. This robot sees everything in its worst possible light. He takes any event or statement as yet further evidence for his very pessimistic views on what others think of him and, indeed, the universe in general. Marvin is thus adept at ignoring the good and positive and focusing on the negative. Not surprisingly, thinking in the ways he does, this poor android is chronically depressed. A few samples:

"You don't have to pretend to be interested in me."
"But I'm quite used to being humiliated. I can even go and stick my head in a bucket of water if you like."
"Life. Don't talk to me of life."
"I think you ought to know I'm feeling very depressed."
"Hey, Marvin," said Zaphod ". . . are we pleased to see you." "No you're not," he said, "no one ever is."
"The first ten million years were the worst . . . and the second ten million years, they were the worst too. The third ten million I didn't enjoy at all. After that I went into a bit of a decline . . . It's the people you meet in this job that really get you down." [From Adams, 1980; 1982.]

Marvin has a negative mental set, a negative style of thinking. His artificial mind is always poised, set to take in some kinds of information (those which support his pessimistic beliefs) and to ignore those that do not. His set therefore makes him misperceive how things really are and leads to some basic errors in thinking which, as we will see, are quite common among people prone to depression.

One can have other mental sets as well, which involve different thinking errors. A common one is a defensive set, in which a person sees threats and danger everywhere. Harmless comments from others get taken as criticism, as threats to self-esteem. Such a person often treads warily through the world, walking with great trepidation. A related set predisposes to quick anger, finding slights, insults and provocations in relatively innocent remarks and actions.

We can have even more general sets, which have a far-reaching impact on our lives. A basic one is "locus of control", described in Chapter 6. As mentioned there, people with an internal locus of control tend to see themselves as having control over events in their lives. Things that happen to them are seen more as the result of their own efforts, skills, abilities and so on. Externals, on the other hand, see themselves more as victims of fate and chance, and believe that there is little they can really do to affect what happens to them.

It is easy to see how having the wrong mental set can greatly intensify the stress a person suffers. One's model of the world might be slightly awry, such that one appraises many harmless events as stressors; as threats or provocations. While the mind can do much to relieve emotional suffering (as with defence mechanisms), a faulty appraisal mechanism may mean the mind itself is the cause of much stress. This notion has been known for many centuries. The ancient Greek philosopher Epictetus put it as follows, "Men are not moved by events but by the views that they take of them". And Shakespeare, speaking through Hamlet, said, "There is nothing good nor bad but that thinking makes it so".

In addition, misperceiving reality usually means a person will be poorly adjusted to it. While seeing things all too clearly may be rather stressful (poets and writers often say "A life without illusion would be intolerable"), viewing them through too-smoky lenses ultimately may mean worse stress.

So, consistently making certain errors in thinking, having particular mental sets and irrational assumptions may create discord, disharmony and an overall lack of realistic adaptation. In this chapter we look at some common thinking errors and suggest some techniques to overcome them, to keep one's perceptions more in line with reality.

HOLDING IRRATIONAL BELIEFS

Psychologist Albert Ellis has very forcefully argued that most human emotional disturbances (he says ninety per cent!) are due to people holding and acting on some common irrational thoughts. These irrational beliefs he says are universal, all of us being susceptible to holding them. Humanity, says Ellis, is biologically predisposed towards irrationality, but can with effort overcome this tendency. Here are some beliefs he lists:

Musturbatory ideology 1: I must do well and win approval for my performances, or else I rate as a rotten person.
Major sub-ideas:
a. I must have sincere love and approval almost all the time from all the people I find significant.
b. I must prove myself thoroughly competent, adequate, and achieving, or at least have real competence or talent at something important.
c. My emotional misery comes almost completely from external pressures that I have little ability to change or control; unless these pressures change, I cannot help making myself feel anxious, depressed, self-downing, or hostile.
d. If events occur that put me in real danger or that threaten my life, I have to make myself exceptionally preoccupied with and upset about them.
e. My past life influenced me immensely and remains all-important because if something once strongly affected me it has to keep determining my feelings and behavior today; my early childhood gullibility and conditionability still remains, and I cannot surmount it and think for myself.
f. I must have a high degree of order or certainty in the universe around me to enable me to feel comfortable and to perform adequately.
g. I desperately need others to rely and depend upon; because I shall always remain so weak, I also need some supernatural power on which to rely, especially in times of severe crisis.
h. I must understand the nature or secret of the universe in order to live happily in it.
i. I can and should give myself a global rating as a human, and I can only rate myself as good or worthy if I perform well, do worthwhile things, and have people generally approve of me.

j. If I make myself depressed, anxious, ashamed, or angry, or I weakly give in to the feelings of disturbance that people and events tend to make me feel, I perform most incompetently and shamefully. I must not do that, and I amount to a thoroughly weak, rotten person if I do.

k. Beliefs held by respected authorities or by my society must prove correct and I have no right to question them in theory or action; if I do, people have a perfect right to condemn and punish me, and I cannot bear their disapproval.

Musturbatory ideology 2: Others must treat me considerately and kindly, in precisely the way I want them to treat me; if they don't, society and the universe should severely blame, damn, and punish them for their inconsiderateness.

Major sub-ideas:

a. Others must treat everyone in a fair and just manner; and if they act unfairly or unethically they amount to rotten people, deserve damnation and severe punishment, and the universe will almost certainly see that they get this kind of retribution.

b. If others behave incompetently or stupidly, they turn into complete idiots and ought to feel thoroughly ashamed of themselves.

c. If people have the ability to do well but actually choose to shirk and avoid the responsibilities they should accept and carry out, they amount to rotters and should feel utterly ashamed of themselves. People must achieve their full potential for happy and worthwhile living, else they have little or no value as humans.

Musturbatory ideology 3: Conditions under which I live must be arranged so that I get practically everything I want comfortably, quickly, and easily, and get virtually nothing that I don't want.

Major sub-ideas:

a. Things must go the way I would like them to go, because I need what I want; and life proves awful, terrible, and horrible when I do not get what I prefer.

b. When dangers or fearsome people or things exist in my world, I must continually preoccupy myself with and upset myself about them; in that way I will have the power to control or change them.

c. I find it easier to avoid facing many of life's difficulties and self-responsibilities than to undertake more rewarding forms of self-discipline. I need immediate comfort and cannot go through present pain to achieve future gain.

d. People should act better than they usually do; and if they don't act well and do create needless problems for me, I view it as awful and horrible and I can't stand the hassles that they then create.

e. Once handicaps exist in my life, either because of my hereditary tendencies or the influences of my past or present environment, I can do practically nothing to change them; I must continue to suffer endlessly because of these handicaps. Therefore life hardly seems worth continuing.

f. If changing some obnoxious or handicapping element in myself or my life proves hard, that difficulty ought not to exist. I find it too hard to do anything about it; I might as well make no effort, or very little effort, to change it.

g. Things like justice, fairness, equality, and democracy clearly have to prevail; when they don't, I can't stand it and life seems too unbearable to continue.

h. I must find correct and practically perfect solutions to my problems and others' problems; if I don't, catastrophe and horror will result.

i. People and external events cause practically all my unhappiness and I have to remain a helpless victim of anxiety, depression, feelings of inadequacy, and hostility unless these conditions and people change and allow me to stop feeling disturbed.

j. Since I managed to get born and now remain alive, my life has to continue forever, or just about as long as I want it to continue. I find it completely unfair and horrible to think about the possibility of my dying and no longer having any existence.

k. As long as I remain alive, my life has to have some unusual or special meaning or purpose; if I cannot create this meaning or purpose for myself, the universe or some supernatural force in the universe must give it to me.

l. I can't stand the discomfort of feeling anxious, depressed, guilty, ashamed, or otherwise emotionally upset; if I really went crazy and wound up in a mental institution, I never could stand that horror and might well have to kill myself.

m. When things have really gone bad for me for a reasonably long period of time and no guarantee exists that they will change or that anyone will take over my life and make things better for me, I simply can't bear the thought of living any longer and have to seriously consider killing myself. [From Ellis, 1977.]

It is easy to see how holding such beliefs can lead to unhappiness and too much stress. For example, consider the one about needing sincere love and approval from everyone significant at all times. Inevitably, this will just not happen. Sometimes one will be out of favor. Some significant person simply may not like one (often for the very reasons that others *do*), and the gap between the belief and the reality will always be there. So emotional strain may result. In the same way, the belief that life will be awful if things do not go as we wish can have a malign effect. Inevitably, sometimes things won't. (Recall Murphy's Law: If anything can go wrong, it will, and at the worst possible time.) So, instead of seeing such events as catastrophic and terrible and becoming overwrought, see them as regrettable but unavoidable inconveniences.

From such irrational beliefs one can get chains of faulty logic which lead to more stress-inducing thoughts. For example, let us say that a man's wife has just left him and he concludes that no one loves him. He holds the irrational assumption that he cannot live without love, and this leads to further conclusions. Since no one loves him and he cannot live without love, he is worthless, a burden on everyone and might as well be dead. And great depression may result from this morose reasoning.

Ellis prescribes a cure for such irrational thinking called rational–emotive therapy, or RET for short. Its use involves using the four Ds: detecting, debating, discriminating and defining.

Detecting first consists of knowing well the possible irrational thoughts and looking for them in one's own thinking. Start with an event or situation that causes you some emotional upset. Then, think back over it, try to detect the specific thoughts that arose as its start and map out the chain of logic which leads to faulty conclusions. *Debating* means to question the kinds of beliefs one has that seem to produce an upset. One questions, for instance, whether event A is really a catastrophe; for example, whether it is impossible to live without love or lots of money. You continually hammer away at such beliefs. Act like a scientist and ask for evidence to support them, for examples to show their truth. As Ellis puts it, "What evidence supports it? In which way does it have truth — or falseness? What makes it so?" And if indeed you find little or no evidence, like a good scientist toss out the belief and look for a better one.

Discriminating means telling the difference between a variety of things; between needs and wants (I *must* be rich versus I *would like* to be rich, I *must* be extremely competent at my job versus I *would like* to be competent); between desires and demands, between sound, rational ideas and irrational ones. It means discriminating faulty logic from sound logic, inconveniences from catastrophes, occurrences that are really just unpleasant from truly unbearable ones. *Defining* is a little more complicated. It means being precise about your terms, giving them all good, short clear definitions, also like a scientist.

Here is a long example of how RET can be used. The following dialogue is between a RET therapist and a woman with an anxiety problem. After a while it became clear that her anxiety tended to occur in public places, especially when eating in restaurants. The therapist then homed in on the specific irrational ideas causing her problem. The debate here was between two people, but there is no reason why one cannot have a similar dialogue with oneself.

CLIENT: *I had another anxiety attack yesterday. I was having lunch with some good friends in this really nice restaurant. I felt like I couldn't finish my meal. It was just terrible.*

THERAPIST: *Okay. Now think back to when you were in the restaurant yesterday, and tell me what you experienced. You know, how you felt and what you were thinking.*

CLIENT: *Okay ... Well, the waiter had just served the main course. I noticed I was really tense. I remember thinking ... "What if I have another panic attack, right here? I might not be able to continue eating. I might even faint. That would be terrible."*

THERAPIST: *Well, you said that you've never actually fainted in situations like this before. And so my guess is you won't ... but what if you did? How would it be terrible? Do you mean* that you would injure yourself physically or something like that?

CLIENT: No ... not really. I think I imagine myself, you know, slumped over in my chair. And my friends and everybody else are looking at me, just staring.

THERAPIST: And what are those people thinking?

CLIENT: That ... I can't even have lunch without making an ass of myself ... that I'm incompetent ... worthless.

THERAPIST: I can see that thinking in that way makes you very tense. Let's try the relaxation technique I taught you. [At this point, the therapist had the client go through three to four minutes of cue-controlled relaxation.]

THERAPIST: How do you feel now?

CLIENT: Better; pretty good.

THERAPIST: Okay. Now it looks to me like you think the worst thing that could happen would be that you'd faint. First, that is pretty unlikely, right?

CLIENT: Sure but what if I did?

THERAPIST: Suppose you were in a restaurant and you saw somebody else faint. What would you think about them? Would you judge them to be incompetent and worthless?

CLIENT: I guess I'd think they were, you know, sick ... I'd probably try to help them. No ... I wouldn't think they were ... bad ... or worthless. I see what you mean. Maybe they wouldn't ridicule me.

THERAPIST: I think they wouldn't. But suppose they did. There you are, slumped in your chair and you are just regaining consciousness. And everyone in the restaurant ... your friends ... everyone ... they are jeering you ... they are making fun of you. We just agreed that isn't likely to happen, but suppose everybody in the restaurant just happened to behave like purple meanies.

CLIENT: That would be awful ... I couldn't stand it. I'd just wither up and die.

THERAPIST: You'd literally physically wither up and die?

CLIENT: Well, when you put it that way ... I guess not. I'd feel terrible, though.

THERAPIST: Remember the A−B−C thing we discussed last week? A is people jeering after you've fainted, C is your reaction.

145

True, most people in that situation wouldn't feel very good. But how bad, how crummy you feel depends on what you choose to say to yourself at B.

CLIENT: *That I'm a worthless nothing who can't even handle herself in a restaurant!*

THERAPIST: *Not so fast. Let's talk about this idea of worthwhileness. If you and I agree that just because you passed out and people around you don't approve doesn't have any bearing on your worth, tell me how it is terrible?*

CLIENT: *Well ... people should be able to handle themselves!*

THERAPIST: *Guess what, Helen ... you just musturbated.*

CLIENT: *(Looks shocked, then laughs) What do you mean?*

THERAPIST: *You said people should do such and such ... like, people must do such and such ... that's where the term musturbation comes from. The thing is this: As children we are taught we should do this, or we must do that, or we shouldn't do this. And we grow up accepting this without ever thinking about it logically. The reality is that the "shoulds" and "musts" are the rules that other people hand down to us, and we grow up accepting them as if they are absolute truth, which they most assuredly aren't.*

CLIENT: *You mean it is perfectly okay to, you know, pass out in a restaurant?*

THERAPIST: *Sure!*

CLIENT: *But ... now I'm confused ... I know I wouldn't like it to happen.*

THERAPIST: *I can certainly understand that. It would be unpleasant, awkward, inconvenient. But it is illogical and irrational to think that it would be terrible, or that you shouldn't or that it somehow bears on your worth as a person. Thinking this way is also very self-defeating.*

CLIENT: *What do you mean?*

THERAPIST: *Well, suppose one of your friends calls you up and invites you back to that restaurant. If you start telling yourself, "I might panic and pass out and people might make fun of me and that would be terrible," you are going to make yourself uptight. And you might find you are dreading going to the restaurant, and you probably won't enjoy the meal very much.*

CLIENT: *Well, that is what usually happens.*

THERAPIST: *But it doesn't have to be that way. That is the really important thing. Remember the A—B—Cs. The way you feel, your reaction, C, depends on what you choose to believe or think, or say to yourself, at B. A could be anything. Like your friend inviting you to meet her at the restaurant. Or noticing you are tense when the meal is being served.*

CLIENT: *Well, what should I think, Doctor?*

THERAPIST: *That was a musturbation! Can you state that in a more rational way?*

CLIENT: *(Laughs) Hmmm . . . let's see. What would be a . . . healthy . . . thing to think?*

THERAPIST: *Let's role-play it. I'll be your friend calling you up to invite you to the restaurant. Then you say aloud the thoughts that you might think that would be, well, healthy, to use your word. [From Rimm & Masters, 1979.]*

The RET approach is more detailed than can be squeezed in here. But, Albert Ellis has written many books on RET, and how his ideas can be applied in several spheres of life. Many of his books are aimed at a general audience and a list of some is at this chapter's end.

EGOIZING

This quite common thinking error has been described in detail by Arnold Lazarus (1977). It means continually putting one's self, one's ego on the line in a whole range of situations. This fault, argues Lazarus, may be responsible for much of the guilt, anxiety and depression that people suffer from. One has an overgeneralized self, an ego that is pretty much the same across all situations. And from this, one generalizes from one or two situations to all. For example, let us say one fails in one or two spheres of life, say marriage or a job, for whatever reason. From this, a person says, "I am a failure!" This implies a failure not just at that particular job (or whatever) but at everything; a failure in all walks of life. It implies a null value as a father, friend, leisure-taker, and general human being.

Lazarus tells of a case of a professional man whose job required much public speaking, which created lots of anxiety for him. As it turned out, this seemed to be because of a great fear of failure. Failure at speaking to a crowd meant failure at his job, which meant failure at life. So, whenever he gave a talk his entire worth as a human being hinged on his success. No wonder he was anxious! But a much better way to live is to see life as consisting of many different spheres. Thus, one can fail at one or more, but still succeed in others.

Egoizing is a frequent error in dating and courtship. Many people take rejection by a prospective partner not for what it often is; just that that person was either not for them or was feeling off because of some reason that had nothing to do with them. It gets taken as a complete rejection of oneself as a human being. Indeed that is why many people are extremely anxious when asking a particular person for a date. Their whole being rests on the result.

The counter to this kind of thinking error is to try to separate one's ego from every single situation. See yourself not as one big ego who is the same across all situations, who is identical in all spheres of life. See yourself as a variety of different egos in different situations. All of us are changeable across circumstances, of course. This strategy can be summed up as the "little i" technique, described by Lazarus. See yourself not as one big I constant in all realms, but as a whole series of little i's, one for each sphere.

ERRONEOUS THINKING STYLES

The last two sections looked at some more-or-less universal irrational ideas, maladaptive beliefs or habits that many of us seem to be prone to. In this section, we look at some maladaptive *styles* of thinking, sets like Marvin's. These are particular ways of distorting reality, chronic ways of misperceiving and misthinking about the world which can lead to a poor adjustment and stress.

Aaron Beck (1976) has listed many such thinking errors. Before describing these, let us first consider three major points that Beck makes. First, he notes, as indeed many an experimental psychologist can vouch for, that perception does not equal reality. The way that we look at the world is not the way the world actually is. This is an extremely important point that many of us often just do not realize. We indeed always select out some things to perceive and ignore others, depending on our motivation, mood, personality and so on. Second, the way that we do interpret reality depends largely on the way that we think, a point that will become clearer soon. Third, our beliefs are not unshakeable, eternal truths as many of us often believe. They are best regarded as hypotheses, propositions that may or may not be right. They can be tested against reality for their correctness. (Ellis also made this point.) So, even our most clearly cherished beliefs (that we *must* work, are incompetent in certain situations, that we are almost always right, and so on) may not be correct and can be tested.

Bedrosian and Beck (1980) also list these thinking errors. This list in many ways to me seems like a summary of some aspects of human nature.

THINKING IN BLACK AND WHITE   This is seeing all events in extreme terms, never seeing the shades of grey in between. So, all people may be labelled as either good or bad, never anything in between. One is either a success or a failure, a good spouse or parent or a bad one. Other people either love us or hate us. They are either friends or enemies. Beck tells of a young man who took everyone he met as either completely rejecting him or completely accepting him. If it was rejection, he quickly got depressed. He apparently could not see that there were many shades of feeling between these two extremes.

OVERGENERALIZING   When we generalize, we go from one small piece of information to a more general statement about the world. If one side of a house is red, we usually infer that the other side is too. If a person is very aggressive in one or two situations, we usually generalize from that that he will probably be pretty fierce in others as well. Overgeneralizing is going from one small piece of information to a big, blanket conclusion that does not really follow. For example, a person making a small mistake on the job may generalize from this to the conclusion that he is hopeless at his work and should be fired. A person who bores another on one occasion (who may have something different weighing on his mind anyway) may overgeneralize this to mean "I am a very dull person". A small snub from another may be taken as evidence that everyone dislikes one.

MAGNIFICATION AND EXAGGERATION   This also involves making very extreme judgments. Here one expects the very worst, most dire consequences to occur in a given situation. One magnifies the danger, the chances of calamity, out of all proportion. A person about to board a plane might dwell only on the chance of crashing, even if the possibility is very slim indeed. A student about to take an exam may expect the very worst possible grade.

ARBITRARY INFERENCE   This error is drawing a conclusion from very little sound data at all. Basically one has a response set, to interpret virtually anything in terms of one already-made conclusion. Again, this is basically Marvin's problem. He concludes from anything that no one likes him and that the universe and life in general are bad.

ASSUMING TOO MUCH PERSONAL RESPONSIBILITY Many overestimate the extent to which a variety of different events are due somehow to them. A person tends to blame his own perceived faults, shortcomings and acts for events that really were not caused by him. For example, the boss might walk past without saying "hello" because he is deeply immersed in thought. But, a person might interpret this as a snub due to something he has done.

BAD JUDGMENT OF SAFETY AND DANGER   We face two major kinds of danger at certain times. One type is purely physical; being run over by a bus, punched in the nose, falling off a ladder. The other type is social; being insulted, humiliated, having self-esteem lowered by others, being ostracized, or offending the powers that be and not getting promoted or even being fired. Much of our thinking and behavior is taken up with finding ways to avoid or minimize both sorts of danger. And to do this, we need a good sense of what may lead to harm and what may not. Beck argues that some people consistently overestimate the risk in certain situations, and so are often anxious, may avoid much and lead a fairly restricted life. Agoraphobics are good examples, being afraid to leave the house because of supposedly dangerous things lurking outside. The reverse side of this coin is a person who consistently underestimates danger. As a result, he or she may have problems dealing with others, and may suffer many accidents as well.

An interesting example of such a person is one of the concentration-camp survivors described in Chapter 4. He lost his sense of danger the day of arrival at the camp and it stayed lost in his post-war life. He worked at a government agency and came into frequent conflict with co-workers.

I spoke out against them and the director came. We argued and he fired me ... The psychiatrist pointed out that I was insulting powerful men in the government who could do me great harm. In a sense it is true; I don't feel the right proportion between the danger and the consequences. [From Dimsdale, 1974.]

SETTING UNREALISTIC GOALS   We all have goals in life. They can range from rising to the top of our profession, securing a comfortable house in the suburbs, becoming rich, making some small contribution to humanity, to getting a university degree. However, many people particularly prone to too much stress may set very unrealistic ones, ones that they have little or no hope of ever achieving. Either the goals may just be far beyond their ability, their raw talent, or they simply depend too much on luck. Examples are becoming a very prominent writer or scientist, a world-famous movie star, or a head of government. So a person's time and energy may be much taken up in striving for an impossible goal, with much stress as a result. When it finally becomes clear that the goal will never be attained, great depression can set in. The solution of course is to set realistic aims within one's potential. Trying to live up to media images (of beauty, wealth, family harmony etc.) may have a similar effect.

OBEYING THE "SHOULDS"   These are rules of conduct which get ground into us when we are children. They are unrealistic standards, rules that no one can really live up to. Yet people often feel they must, and the "shoulds" can act like little internal tyrants, always driving us onwards. They run along the lines of "I should always be perfect" or "always happy". To summarize, "I should always be a superhuman". Since these standards are far too rarefied for anyone to meet, continually trying to may set the stage for much anxiety and depression when one fails. They are closely akin to some of Ellis's irrational assumptions.

Consistently making such thinking errors as the above can lead not just to faulty perceptions and sets but to wholly inaccurate *belief systems*. Let us digress for just a moment to elaborate on this concept a little. A belief system is a personal way of looking out at the world, interpreting what happens in it, a set of beliefs about what reality is and what causes what in it. For example, consider the belief system of a hypothetical Indian living a primitive life in the Amazon forest. Say that he has never seen any signs of civilization at all. He may believe that the entire world is forest, not being able to imagine anything else. He may believe that his tiny tribe is all of humanity, that the sun and moon go around the Earth, and that the world is populated by many spirits. Some of the extreme forms of Christianity are another example. Some of their tenets are that the world is a kind of testing ground for humanity, that we are here for one lifetime to be judged and then sent to heaven or hell.

The above are systems held by a number of people in common, but many people have personal belief systems that may be very out of line with reality. For example, Beck tells of a man whose wife had just left him and who was very depressed as a result. He stayed that way because his system of beliefs included some that really were inaccurate; "She is the mainstay of my life", "I can never live without her". From these beliefs others follow; that he can never be happy without her, and finally that he might as well be dead. But, objectively, such views are wrong. A favorite trick of Beck's was to ask such a person if he had been happy before he met his wife, and usually the answer was "yes". Much suffering might be avoided by bringing one's system of beliefs more in line with commonsense. The philosopher Immanuel Kant felt that replacing ordinary commonsense with such a "private sense" was responsible for all emotional disturbances.

Beck gives some interesting ways to try to free oneself from the slavery such errors in thinking as the above can lead to. First, as with Ellis's irrational ideas, one should be aware of the possible errors we are prone to make. Second is to act like a scientist. As mentioned earlier, one should accept that even one's more cherished beliefs may not be true. They should be treated as hypotheses open to test, tests against reality. Beck gives an interesting but extreme case of this method. A man suffering from depression had not left his bed for a year. He said that he could not stand up at all, that he would fall, and therefore must remain in bed. Beck offered him a chance to test this dearly held belief, promising to catch him if he did indeed fall. After much persuasion the man agreed, discovered that his belief was wrong and that he really could stand, and in fact was walking around by himself soon after. Another extreme example is a woman who mistakenly felt that she would be rejected by just about everyone. How did she know this? By ESP, was the reply. She could tell what others were thinking and knew they would reject her. So, she was offered a chance to test this idea out through a Rhine-type card-reading task. She had to guess what card the therapist was holding. Her ESP score was zero, and she scored the same when trying out the experiment with her husband later.

Another of Beck's methods is *distancing*. The idea here is to try to refine your thoughts about something, to make clear and explicit all your assumptions. For example, Beck tells of a middle-aged scientist who felt that he was a failure at his job. The latter is a quite general blanket judgment that needs refining. So, in what areas was he failing to carry out his work? What was expected of him and how was he not meeting those expectations? Were there some aspects of his job in which he was doing well? What feedback had he received from superiors and colleagues? Many blanket judgments cannot survive this kind of specificity; their unsound basis becomes clear. As it turned out, in this case there was very little support for his negative self-view. Beck gives another example; a young wife complaining of feeling inferior to her more successful husband. She was worried that he would abandon her for a more interesting co-worker, with whom he would have more in common. But, just why her husband would prefer someone else to her she was rather vague about. So, distancing was applied. She had to list all the ways in which she and her husband shared common interests and values. There were indeed many, occurring in most spheres of life. When her husband later put together his own list, the two were astonishingly similar.

Another method is *decentring*. This means prying oneself loose from the mistaken notion that one is the centre of all events, or at least of a great many. Again, people particularly prone to depression often have this, quite seriously believing that fate has somehow singled them out for special attention to make their life as miserable as possible. Many who are anxious in social or crowd situations often have the mistaken notion that everyone is watching them, or that everyone can see how tense they are. As well, many feel that no one else ever has their particular difficulty; for example, that no one else is uncomfortable in the situations in which they are. How does one decentre? First, by keeping all senses open, by looking around, asking people about their own reactions and feelings, getting more information about the lives and problems of others. These frequently reveal an astonishing similarity to one's own.

Decatastrophizing we saw to some extent in the dialogue earlier in this chapter. Catastrophizing is saying "this is awful and unbearable", or predicting the very worst consequences for an event. Beck gives an example of a student who had to give a talk being paralyzed by the thought of public speaking. He had a morbid fear of appearing foolish, believing that he could never live such a catastrophic experience down. Decatastrophizing is looking ahead, working through one's assumptions and their consequences. What would indeed happen if my worst expectations came true? Could I never live it down? Would my career and life come to an end? In the above example, the student was asked whether, even if he did give a bad talk, he really believed no one would ever speak to him again without laughing? For how long would he feel terrible? Had anything like this happened to him before, and if so, how long did the trauma afterward actually last? From such questioning and thinking through, one may come to see that a particular event is being given far too much significance, that one is losing perspective.

The final method to be described here is *reattributing responsibility*. Again, a cause of great stress which can lead to overanxiety or depression is blaming oneself for many events that are really due to other factors. The causes of events are misattributed to oneself. The solution is to review all one knows about a negative situation, collect more data if necessary and try to see just what is leading to what, how much of the causes if any are due to oneself. Beck gives an example of a lawyer very concerned about a coming court case. He saw himself as totally responsible for the way the verdict went, and was very worried about his presentation of the case. So, he compiled a chart which estimated just how much influence many other factors had; the judge, the jury, the quality of the opposing side's arguments and so on. Sure enough, the contribution of his own presentation was rated as pretty small.

OVERCOMING BELIEFS IN PERSONAL INEFFECTIVENESS

We saw in Chapter 6 that to believe in one's ability to deal with, to master situations, in one's self-efficacy, is very important in coping. Feeling the opposite, that one is helpless, or lacks the power or skill to gain given ends in certain situations, is often a grave thinking error. A major goal of the second half of this book is to give coping techniques whose use may strengthen feelings of self-efficacy. Developing good coping and problem-solving skills, seeing them work in many different situations, does much to help. The ability to relax, to control anxiety, to become less emotional in previously difficult circumstances, also helps promote efficacy feelings. Most of us indeed know that our ability to perform well plummets when we are too aroused.

In this section we look at some further methods of promoting efficacy feelings, put forward by Goldfried and Robins (1982). But first, to fully understand how they work, we need to look more closely at the idea of a self-concept.

Each of us has a particular image of self, of what we are like, what character traits we have, what our capabilities, faults and strengths are, and how we respond to different situations and people. Even animals such as apes have some idea of self. (This was shown in an experiment in which an ape was anaesthetized and a large red spot painted on its forehead. When the animal awoke, it was given a mirror and when the ape saw its reflection its hand immediately shot up to the red spot.) We use our self-image to understand experiences, why others react to us as they do. For example, a person who sees himself as unattractive, rather timid, and physically weak will use this image to understand why surfers kick sand in his face at the beach, why he has trouble getting a date on Saturday night, and why many people pay little attention to him. All these events fit in with his self-concept. Similarly, a person who sees himself as powerless, and lacking in many important social skills may not try to directly cope with his difficulties. He may avoid many situations that his self-image tells him he cannot handle.

But, while there may be a grain of truth in such self-views, often they are far from accurate. Misperception can operate. One can build up a self-image that includes being personally ineffective and subject to the whims of luck and fate. Such a belief may be maintained by selective perception, our tendencies to see only what fits in with our beliefs and to ignore what does not. Experiences of success and efficacy that do not fit in with our negative self-image may therefore be discounted. Recall Marvin again. He just would not believe that anyone liked him because this did not accord with his negative self-view. Another reason is that one may not be aware of all the environmental forces that push and pull at all of us, as Goldfried and Robins point out. So events really due to external causes are misattributed to our own weaknesses.

An extreme example of such misperception is anorexia nervosa, the slimmer's disease. Young women are most vulnerable. They eat very little at all, often literally wasting away. The causes can be many but often the sufferer sees herself as being overweight and fat, even though objectively she may be very skinny. But the negative self-image of being grossly overweight somehow persists, despite mirrors and feedback from others.

How then can one overcome a self-image that has one as inefficacious? Goldfried and Robins suggest several ways. One is to continually compare your present behavior with your past, before you began learning coping-skill methods. The improvement process can be long and sometimes slow and uncertain. It is therefore a good idea to compare how you recently performed in a stressful situation (with your new knowledge of coping) with how you would have acted in the past, without it. This will often give some rewarding image of improvement, of new-found self-efficacy which may batter away at a negative self-image. Let us say, for example, that you coped quite well in an anger-provoking or anxiety-provoking situation that previously would have given much trouble. Compare the two, noting that you did better.

Another method is to try to assume an objective view of your abilities. Take an observer's stance to watch your performance. Try to see yourself as someone else would. It is an interesting sidelight on human nature that we attribute the causes of behavior differently when an observer than when a participant. People in a situation attribute causes to external factors, while observers find causes inside the heads of the participants. What this can mean is that you as a participant may attribute successful, efficacious events as due to external factors rather than your own efforts. This may be remedied by seeing yourself as a watcher as well.

FURTHER READING

Ellis, A. and Harper, R. A. *A New Guide to Rational Living. N. Hollywood: Wilshire, 1975.*

Ellis, A. Growth Through Reason. Palo Alto: Science & Behavior Books, 1971.

Beck, A. T. *Cognitive Therapy and the Emotional Disorders.* New York: International Universities Press, 1976.

CHAPTER 11

Solving Life Problems

Much of life's stress can be seen as due to daily problems. These curse and plague us all. They can be seemingly minor ones like how to better get on with one's in-laws or spouse's best friend, how to induce oneself to exercise more, how a newlywed housewife might conquer the loneliness she is beginning to feel, how to clear up misunderstandings with a co-worker. The bigger ones can seem more daunting; how a wife might better handle an abusive and sometimes violent husband, how a mother might get her child to labor upon his schoolwork, how to gain promotion at work. Such problems exist when we have a goal (as those above) but no obvious way to reach it. Our old, automatic ways of gaining our ends do not seem to work. Miller, Galanter and Pribram (1960) put it well:

In ordinary affairs we usually muddle ahead, doing what is habitual and customary, being slightly puzzled when it some-times fails to give the intended outcome, but not stopping to worry much about the failures because there are too many other things to do. The circumstances conspire against us and we find ourselves caught failing where we must succeed — where we cannot withdraw from the field, or lower our self-imposed standards, or ask for help, or throw a tantrum. Then we may begin to suspect we face a problem.

Our well-being, our adjustment to our life situation, largely depends on how well we deal with such problems. Poor problem-solving powers can lead to faulty adjustment and much emotional distress for several reasons. First, one may consistently pick the wrong solutions to one's problems. A young girl might, for example, try to solve the problem of exiting from an unhappy household by marrying virtually the first prospective husband to come along. A bout of restlessness on the job due to a midlife crisis might be dealt with by quitting, selling the house, leaving the family and switching to an alternative lifestyle. For some, this answer might work out well but for others catastrophe could be just around the corner. Second, trouble can arise when one either cannot or will not recognize life's problems. Difficulties then may be neglected either from laziness, complacency or sheer unwillingness to act. And small problems tend to snowball over time. Thus a person will not only be landed with the stress of small ones but may be later hit with a very large one. This may well be the story of many a failed marriage. Like all marriages, a doomed one at the start typically has adjustment problems (as mentioned in Chapter 3), such as annoying habits in either or both partners, lack of enough display of affection, or in-law trouble. If these are not recognized and some compromises early on worked out, tension can build up which after months or years may come to a cataclysmic head. One partner may even greet the end with total surprise despite many pointers along the way to the likely finale.

Among the worst problem-solvers of all seem to be many people who try to commit suicide. They tend to have much trouble finding answers to their difficulties and in the end may just see one, to exit from life altogether.

Direct-action problem-solving steps are an important means of dealing with stressors. As the philosopher Socrates said several thousand years ago, "The competent manage well their daily problems and have judgment". Despite its crucial importance, though, this is a skill that we learn haphazardly, if at all. In a variety of different disciplines, new initiates are more or less taught to solve the specific problems arising in that field. Scientists learn to solve scientific problems, managers their problems in industry, and psychotherapists to help solve other people's. Yet until the last decade or so, there has been no systematic effort to teach people to solve their own everyday social problems. Recently, however, several such programmes have been developed. These have drawn ideas from problem-solving instruction in the above fields and the long history of research on it in experimental psychology. Some psychologists are even helping schools teach these skills to children.

The programme described here is drawn from the above sources and some specific social problem-solving training procedures, notably those of Meichenbaum (1977), Spivack, Platt and Shure (1976), Goldfried and Goldfried (1975), and D'Zurilla and Nezu (1982). The programme stresses solving problems by thinking through them in five distinct phases. These phases in practice may overlap, and you may go from a later one back to an earlier one. But, the general method of going through them is a sound approach. Each is described in turn.

STAGE 1: DEVELOP A PROBLEM-SOLVING SET

Just as one can have a set to be defensive or depressed or to anger easily, one can have a set to solve problems. This is much more useful than any other kind. It is a frame of mind, a perspective from which one looks at everyday difficulties. One acknowledges that problems are an inevitable part of life, that at any one time we all have a multitude of small and large ones that need to be attacked. Everyone has them. And one sees that some difficulties simply cannot be avoided, that they are due to human nature. As people come together to live and work, some will inevitably rub others up the wrong way, they will retaliate, some people will seek more power and status and trample others on the way to it, others will try to stop them. Certain situations are ready-made to create certain problems. This is just human nature. And one recognizes that oneself has certain weaknesses which may lead to difficulties in particular circumstances. When one therefore does recognize a problem, one thinks rationally about it, does not catastrophize, does not say "Oh, this is just awful, this is the worst thing that could possibly happen, I just cannot cope". One sees hassles as an unavoidable part of living.

Also part of the set is to learn to identify troublesome situations as problems. The rule of thumb seems to be that if you feel unhappy or emotional about something, then a problem is lurking in the background somewhere. They can often be detected by monitoring yourself over a week or two. For example, if the symptom is depression, ask if it occurs at certain times, such as when lonely or when a particular person is around? Certain patterns may become clear when actually recorded as they

160

happen. Another part of the set is to realize that problems often have good solutions. If they are tackled systematically and some answer applied, they can usually be dealt with. Also try to see yourself as indeed being capable of dealing with them. Avoid a set of negative self-statements or a mistaken sense of inefficacy.

The final part of the set is simply to remember to use one's head. It is very important to think problems through and not act impulsively. The first apparent solution is rarely the best. A hasty, injudicious action may set the stage for much future trouble.

Spivack *et al.* tell an enlightening story about the results of such impulsiveness. One of them was working at a centre for delinquent children. One night, a child broke out of detention to buy something in town. But, since this act was against the house rules, the consequences upon his return were quite dire. And besides this, the shops were closed that late at night, which he would have realized with a little thought. Yet, still he went. Apparently the child just did not think about the likely results of his action at all. He wanted something and adopted an instant but faulty way of trying to get it. Just a little thought would have spared him much trouble.

STAGE 2: DEFINE THE PROBLEM CLEARLY

A sage once said that a problem well-defined is half-solved. There is much truth to this statement. Indeed, before any difficulty can really be tackled, one must clearly understand exactly what the problem is.

For example, consider a married couple who have a lot of tiffs which they find destructive and want to avoid. Exactly what causes the fights has to be precisely defined. Is it a basic incompatibility due to totally different interests and beliefs? If so, divorce might be the best answer. Or, is it a failure to communicate, to pick up the other's messages, which leads to misunderstandings and thus battle? Or, is it simply a temporary external factor like lack of money or some frequently visiting friends of one partner whom the other does not like? If so, the situation may resolve itself with a little time. In every case, though, the solution is different. Unless the problem is well-understood, the wrong answer to it may be adopted.

As another example, consider the problem "How can I reduce the stress I am undergoing and cope better?" Again the best solution will depend on the exact cause; are there some extraordinary stress sources which need to be eliminated or will some strengthening of my own coping powers be enough?

Good problem definition is helped by several actions. First, get all the facts you can about the problem. Get them from other people, from the library. Reading this book will, for example, help in learning many essential facts. The more you can gather the better. Also ask if you have encountered a similar problem before or if someone else has. How was that one solved? Just consider the relevant facts. Leave out one's opinions, assumptions, and biases. These only get in the way.

Another aid to definition is to break large problems into several smaller ones. These are easier to understand and solve. For example, consider the problem "How can I be happier?" As is, the question is hard to tackle. But it can be broken down into:
What do I need to make myself happier?
1. More friends. (How can I make more friends?)
2. More money. (How can I make more money?)
3. A belief that I am getting somewhere in life.
4. Better relations with relatives and neighbors. (How can I improve these?)
5. Better health.

As another example, consider the problem "How can I acquire a spouse?" This might be broken down to:
1. How can I get out and meet more prospective partners?
2. How can I improve my interaction skills?
3. How can I become more attractive to others?

As a further aid to definition, you could use the classification of many problems given by D'Zurilla and Nezu (1982). They see many as falling into four categories. First is *aversion*, where some punishment or aversive event is about to befall. For example, one might be how to make one's home burglary-proof or how to pay one's rent this month to prevent eviction. Second is *loss of reward*. A husband might, for example, try to figure out how to keep his wife, or an individual his job. Third is *frustration*, where there is an obstacle blocking one's clear and straight path to a goal. Fourth is some type of *conflict*. Examples are husband and wife disagreeing on the timing of their first child or about the career plans of one.

When the problem is defined, next specify your goal in solving it. Is the aim simply to relieve distress, to promote a more harmonious relationship, to change certain behavior, or to remove a particular obstacle? State the goal in precise concrete terms and make sure that you really can attain it. As we saw last chapter, setting unrealistic goals can be the source of much stress.

STAGE 3: LIST POSSIBLE SOLUTIONS

Now begins a creative phase. Once your problem is clearly defined, when it seems clear what it is, the next step is to list some answers. Just about every problem has more than one solution and here you let your mind relax and wander and write down all the ones that occur. It is critical here not to evaluate them as you go, just reel them off without considering how well each would work; that comes later. Keep the solutions specific; very general ones may not be much help. For example, for the problem "How can I do better at school or university?" the solution "improve study habits" is too vague and general. Specify how study habits could be improved; for example, by studying to a schedule, studying for a set number of hours, reading textbooks more carefully, taking more detailed lecture notes and so on.

One particularly fine example of a creative solution to a problem was given by then US Treasury Secretary Michael Blumenthal. After dining at a plush San Francisco restaurant, he was presented with the bill and gave a cheque. But he had no extra verification of his signature on the cheque and the waiter was reluctant to take it. The Treasurer's solution: He pulled a newly minted dollar note from his wallet and pointed out his own engraved signature.

A useful technique to use at the solution-generating phase is A. F. Osborn's "brainstorming". This method was developed for use in advertising agencies to think up ideas, better ways to persuade consumers to buy objects that they at present do not want or need. You simply list solutions quickly, off the top of your head. It is extremely important not to evaluate them as you go; that will stop the free flow of thought. Separation of solutions and evaluations is paramount. The presence of others may help here too since that can stimulate creativity.

One can also use the "strategy-tactics" method described by D'Zurilla and Nezu (1982). A strategy is a general approach to solving a problem, and tactics are the specific steps taken to implement it. For example, in World War II, one German strategy was to bring the British to their knees by starving them of vital supplies. That was the general approach which was implemented in particular by using U-boats to sink merchant ships. On the more mundane level of everyday life, one can list some general strategies for resolving some problem and then list tactics to implement it.

To illustrate the solution-generating process, here are a couple of examples. Consider first a hypothetical lady with an inconsiderate neighbor who plays his TV loud late into the night. A short talk with him about this is fruitless, so the following solutions might be generated:

1. Move to a quieter apartment.
2. Retaliate in kind; play music and the TV loud when *he* is trying to sleep and perhaps he will eventually compromise.
3. Talk with him again and try to be more persuasive.
4. Do nothing, and hope to get used to the noise.
5. Line the wall with sound-proof tiles.

For the second example, consider the problem "How can I lose weight?" Some possible solutions are:

1. Try another crash diet from a magazine.
2. Have an operation to remove excess fat.
3. Get more exercise and cut out the most offending foods.
4. Get my jaws wired.
5. Do nothing, and accept that I will always be overweight.

Not all of these, of course, are realistic solutions, but they illustrate the technique.

Many people have trouble at this stage: They find it hard to produce solutions. One then appears to be "stuck". This unhappy state was well-described by Robert Pirsig in *Zen and the*

164

Art of Motorcycle Maintenance:

Stuckness. That's what I want to talk about; A screw sticks for example, on a side cover assembly. You check the manual to see if there might be any special cause for this screw to come off so hard but all it says is "Remove the cover plate" ... This is the zero moment of consciousness ... no answer ... It is normal at this point for the fear/anger syndrome to take over and make you want to hammer on that side plate with a chisel, to pound it off with a sledge hammer if necessary ... you need some ideas, some hypotheses.

"Stuckness" can be caused by a number of factors. One is the too great influence of the past. One can get into a particular set, especially if you have solved a series of seemingly similar problems all in the same way. This has been shown again and again in experiments; how a set can stop one seeing an otherwise perfectly obvious solution. For example, stop reading and try attacking the problems in Table 7 in order from 1 to 7.

Table 7

Here is the problem. You have three water jars all of different capacity. Your task is to measure out an exact amount of water. For example, the first problem is "measure out 100 quarts of water given that you have three jars; one that holds 21 quarts, one that holds 127 quarts, and one that holds 3 quarts." You can solve it by filling up the 127-quart jar, then from it pouring off 21 quarts into jar A and then 3 into jar C, emptying jar C and then pouring another 3 into it. That leaves 100 quarts in jar B. Try the others.

Problem No.	Your three jars			Obtain this amount
	A	B	C	
1.	21	127	3	100
2.	14	163	25	99
3.	18	43	10	5
4.	9	42	6	21
5.	20	59	4	31
6.	23	49	3	20
7.	10	36	7	3

Adapted from Psychology of Learning and Memory *by H. C. Ellis, T. L. Bennett, T. G. Daniel and E. J. Rickert. Copyright © 1979 by Wadsworth, Inc. Reprinted by permission of Brooks/Cole Publishing Company, Monterey, California.*

You probably found problem 7 the hardest. The reason is that the first six can be dealt with by the same simple strategy but 7 needs a different tack. You get into a set and waste time trying to apply it to problem 7 and so past experience has a harmful effect. This can happen with everyday problems. A would-be suitor may be continually rejected in wooing a particular girl because he insists on solving the problem of getting her to like him in ways that he has always used rather than trying new ones. A supervisor might handle all problems on the job in the same, but now unsatisfactory, ways that have worked in the past.

Another barrier to producing solutions is too much emotion. Very serious life problems like how to keep a marriage going, whether to change jobs, or whether to break off a relationship may be too emotion-laden for one to think rationally and methodically about them. There is no easy way around this other than to try some relaxation exercises and to try to detach yourself from the emotion.

A final barrier to solution production is setting limits to your thinking, to your perspective. This fault can be illustrated with a favorite trick of counsellors and anyone else who wants to help you "expand your awareness". Try solving the problem in Figure 3. All you have to do is connect up the dots without lifting pencil from paper and without retracing a line. The solution is given in Figure 4 at the end of this chapter on page 174.

Most people struggle with this one because they try to stick within self-imposed borders; the limits of the dots. Once you go

Figure 3 *The dot problem. Connect up all the dots with four straight lines without retracing a line and lifting pencil from paper. Redrawn from Scheerer (1963).*

beyond them, the solution is easy.

Sometimes the finding of answers can be left to the subconscious mind. If no answer comes to mind, leave the problem for a while to let the subconscious work on it. Many great scientific problems have been solved by such incubation. After immersing himself in all the facts and clearly defining the problem, the scientist may get stuck. So he or she leaves the problem for a couple of days and goes fishing, or turns to something else. Then in a flash of insight, at an often odd time, the solution suddenly is revealed. Picture Archimedes in his bathtub suddenly yelling "eureka", or the famous chemist who suddenly saw the structure of the ring-shaped benzene molecule as a snake swallowing its tail.

If, after using the above methods to break blocks — chopping the problem into smaller parts and trying brainstorming and incubating — solutions still come at but a slow trickle, some creative self-statementing may be in order. Meichenbaum (1975) gives this method as a possible antidote to "stuckness". Research by him and others suggests that people who have trouble producing lots of creative solutions may block themselves with negative self-statements. These act as direct barriers to solution-generating, which might otherwise pour forth. They can be ones such as "I can't do this, I am not very creative", "I have had this problem a long time, I just cannot think of any way to solve it", "I am just too anxious to find an answer". Or, perhaps as a defence against failure, a person may say that this is a worthless task and lose interest.

Meichenbaum gives some positive self-statements to use just as in stress-inoculation training. Table 8 gives them.

STAGE 4: PICK THE BEST SOLUTION

Once your list of answers is complete (or hefty) go through them one by one and decide which best solves the problem. This can be the hardest part. Many people fluently produce ideas but fall down when trying to evalute them. A good example is Winston Churchill. A colleague of his once said that the great man was marvellous at listing ideas but less adept at picking the best one.

Indeed, some straight and sound thinking is definitely

Table 8
Examples of self-statements to prompt creativity in solution-finding. (Adapted from Meichenbaum, 1975.)

Set-inducing self-statements

What to do:
Be creative, be unique.
Break away from the obvious, the commonplace.
Think of something no one else will think of.
Just be freewheeling.
If you push yourself you can be creative.
Quantity helps breed quality.

What not to do:
Get rid of internal blocks.
Defer judgments.
Don't worry what others think.
Not a matter of right or wrong.
Don't give the first answer you think of.
No negative self-statements.

What else to do:
You're in a rut; okay, try something new.
Take a rest now: who knows when the ideas will visit again.
Go slow — no hurry — no need to press.
Good, you're getting it.
This is fun.
Release controls; let your mind wander.
Free-associate; let ideas flow.
Relax, just let it happen.
Let your ideas play.
Refer to your experiences; just view it differently.
Feel like a bystander through whom ideas are just flowing.
Let one answer lead to another.
Almost dreamlike, the ideas have a life of their own.

needed at this point. Two major points should be considered. First, how likely is it that a particular solution will work? What are the chances of failure and how serious will failure be? Is a less worthy solution therefore more likely to work and would I be better off trying it? Here you need to peer into the future with an imaginary crystal ball and try to see what might happen. Some understanding of and knowledge of the consequences are needed. Ask also if your solution can be implemented at all.

The second question is what solution is best of those you have listed. This will differ for different situations and different people. Solution A might be ideal for one person and B for another. You therefore need to pick an answer you can live with, one that seems as satisfactory as possible for all concerned, and one that does not conflict with your values. Again it is useful to try to peer into the future and test out the long-term consequences of a particular action. Will it create more problems, harm others, permanently solve the difficulty? Look ahead. This is what a chess grandmaster does when selecting a move, which is solving a problem presented by the particular configuration of pieces on the board. He might consider the consequences of two or three different lines many moves into the future. What will my opponent do? Will this move aid my plan? What sort of position will it lead to?

To illustrate this stage, let us again take up the two examples from the last section. First, we consider the solutions to the loud TV:

Move? Just too much trouble right now and too expensive. Housing is very short in this city, and besides, I like this place very much. I could easily run into noisy, uncooperative neighbors at some other place anyway.

Retaliate? No, this will just inflame the situation and is unpalatable and unlikely to work. Even if it does, it will poison relations between the two of us for a long time to come. Reject that one.

Talk again? This is worth a try if I can do it without getting angry. But it is not likely to work. He says that he is hard of hearing and cannot sleep at night and so watches TV. Neither will he get headphones for it.

Do nothing? It has been going on for a while and it still really bothers me. No, my health is being affected too much.

Some sound-proof tiles? These are expensive but I can afford them now and it will be worth it for my peace of mind. And it will not create any long-term problems because no one else around here but me is involved. Yes, I think this is the best answer.

And the second example:

Try another crash diet? These never work for long. I just suffer for a few weeks and then go on a binge. No one else I know has ever lost weight for long with such a diet.

Have an operation? Very expensive and very risky. No, that kind of heroic effort I can do without.

Get my jaws wired? No, just too horrendous an answer. I could not hold my head up in public and am just not *that* desperate to shed my extra kilograms.

Accept my fate? I suppose that I could resign myself to it, if indeed that is to be my lot in life. But I really am bothered by this excess weight and carrying extra kilograms is risky to health.

Get more exercise and cut out the most offending foods? This might be best. I hate workouts but could keep them up if I can get someone to exercise with me. I could join a health club or organize some friends. And if I take someone along shopping, I could probably avoid the worst of fattening foods. Yes, this is worth a try.

It may help to use a rating-scale method for solution evaluation. Each solution could be rated, using a seven-point scale (with 7 as very good, 6 as good, 4 as neutral, 1 as very bad) according to a number of criteria. Rate the solution as to its likelihood of success, its harm to others, its long-term practicability, how well it fits in with your own values and so on. Then work out an average figure for each solution and pick the one with the highest score.

STAGE 5: VERIFY YOUR SOLUTION

Once the problem has been defined, a solution found and tried, the final step is to verify that it worked. This confirmation usually takes place some time after you have acted. Has the problem been satisfactorily resolved now? Is the solution working out without any undue hassles, or have more problems been created as a result?

If your solution does not seem to be working well, try another. Become an experimenter, testing various answers until you hit upon one that brings success. A good way to remember this phase is with the acronym TOTE, coined by Miller *et al.* (1960). TOTE stands for test-operate-test-exit. You test a solution, try another if it does not work and keep testing until you find one that does. Then, like a computer programme run to completion, you exit from your now-completed problem-solving sequence.

A DETAILED EXAMPLE   Three stages of the problem-solving sequence can be further illustrated by a long example from Goldfried and Goldfried (1975). The first phase is implied and the fifth one not actually mentioned here. A girl with a vague, undefined problem sought help from a counsellor. Their talk illustrates the above steps in solving problems remarkably well:

Definition

CLIENT: *I've been feeling very tired and irritable lately, and sometimes I get very depressed.*

THERAPIST: *How long have you been feeling this way?*

CLIENT: *Oh, for about the past couple of months. I guess it started soon after I moved here and found this new apartment. Actually, I like the apartment very much. It's very convenient to work and restaurants and movies — I mean it's really in a terrific area and fairly safe at night too. The problem is that it's kind of small. The living arrangement is not too good.*

THERAPIST: *In what way do you feel the size of your apartment is related to your upset?*

CLIENT: *Well, it's really a very large studio apartment, but I can't afford the rent by myself, so I have a roommate. That means we have to use that one room as both bedroom and living room and it gets a bit cramped at times.*

THERAPIST: *Are you having trouble getting along with your roommate?*

CLIENT: *No, I don't think that's a problem. I like her and she's friendly and easy to get along with. But you're right. There is one problem with her. Well, maybe it's a problem with me. I have this great new job, which is very challenging and demanding, but it takes a lot out of me and I find I have to get a good night's sleep in order to function. My roommate and her friends are "night people" and like to stay up late talking or listening to records. I really envy her — she also has to get up early and go to work, but she seems to manage on much less sleep than me.*

THERAPIST: *What has been happening?*

CLIENT: *I haven't been getting enough sleep and I feel very tired much of the time. I end up staying up with them and not only do I feel tired, but I'm not too crazy about my roommate's friends. The next morning I'm usually tired and depressed because socializing with people I don't particularly like only points out to me how lonely I am.*

THERAPIST: *So, it's not only that you'd like some other arrangement about the time of night the apartment is free of guests. You'd also like to have more social contacts yourself.*

CLIENT: *Yes, I think that's also part of it. I had some good friends before I moved to the area, but I haven't been able to find anyone around here.*

Solution-generating

THERAPIST: *Now that we have a better idea of what your current problem is, let's investigate some possible solutions. I'd like you to use the brainstorming technique I told you about, where you think of as many possibilities as you can, no matter how silly or impractical they may seem. Let your mind run free.*

CLIENT: *I'll try.*

THERAPIST: *Remember, try to think of as many solutions as possible. You don't really have to carry them all out. And don't worry at this point about being too specific. Later on we'll be concerned about specific solutions to actually carry out. Right now, I'd like you to concentrate on general approaches to the problem.*

CLIENT: *Could you explain what you mean by a general approach.*

THERAPIST: *Well, for example, let's assume that in a particular problematic situation one possible solution was, "I would get a better job". That possible solution is described at a very general level, telling what you would do, but not how you*

172

would go about doing it. The "how to do it" part might involve reading the want ads in the paper every day, calling friends and asking if they know of any job openings, registering with employment agencies, as well as a host of other specific ways of following through the general approach of "get a better job".

CLIENT: *Yes, I understand now.*

THERAPIST: *Good. Now I'd like you to tell me as many possible solutions as you can and I'll write them down. Just let the possibilities come — no matter how silly some may seem. But do keep in mind the two major concerns in your situation: The need for more sleep, and the desire for more friends.*

CLIENT: *Well, I could try and go to sleep even when they're in the room by using earplugs. I could tell her friends to leave at a certain hour. I could ask my roommate to start and end the socializing earlier in the evening. I guess I could just have a good talk with her, explain the problem and work something out together. Maybe we could have people over just on weekends when I could sleep later in the morning. Or we could not have people over at all. Maybe I could find a way to live on less sleep. I know I'll have to find friends of my own so I won't be lonely.*

THERAPIST: *Anything else? What about finding another job that paid more, so you could get a different apartment?*

Evaluation

THERAPIST: *I have here a list of the alternatives you suggested and I'd like you to consider which would be worthwhile pursuing. First of all, are there any not worth bothering with at all?*

CLIENT: *Frankly, I don't think it would be physically possible for me to live on less sleep and still function well. I've always needed about eight hours of sleep a night and I'm in good health otherwise. I just think it's my constitution, and I doubt that it can be changed.*

THERAPIST: *Any others that you want to reject?*

CLIENT: *No.*

THERAPIST: *I'd like you to think about each of these possible solutions in terms of the implications not only for you, but for others around you — friends and family. In addition, think not only of the immediate consequences, but also what the long-term results may be. Why don't we think first about your trying to sleep while people are socializing in the room.*

CLIENT: *I'd probably find the noise more annoying than the light so maybe I could use earplugs, or perhaps one of those machines that have a steady humming sound to blot out the noise. Actually, even if I could get to sleep it seems like a pretty awkward situation and I'm sure it would put a strain on my relationship with my roommate. Maybe I should concentrate on working out an arrangement with my roommate where the apartment is free of guests at my bedtime.*

THERAPIST: *O.K. Let's look at that.*

CLIENT: *One of the things we could do is to have people come over only on weekends. That way I could choose to be home or be out socializing on my own, without worrying about how late it is getting. I'll talk to my roommate and maybe we can come up with something like "house rules". Maybe I'm doing things that she doesn't like and I'd offer to change some of my ways — so it would be a compromise of sorts.*

THERAPIST: *How do you think that would affect your relationship with your roommate?*

CLIENT: *I'm not sure, but she's pretty easygoing, so somehow I think it would be all right. At least it's worth a try.*

THERAPIST: *How would you evaluate this alternative?*

CLIENT: *Good, even very good.*

THERAPIST: *O.K., let's go on to some other alternatives.*

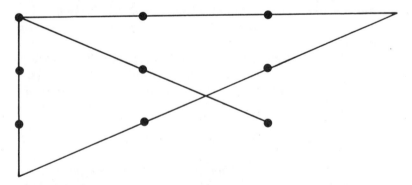

Figure 4 *Solution to the dot problem. Redrawn from Scheerer (1963).*

CHAPTER 12

Overcoming Barriers to Personal Change

Human beings often stubbornly resist making needed changes in habits and lifestyle. We keep up unhealthy behaviors like smoking, eating and drinking too much, and driving danger-ously. We cling to old, faulty ways of dealing with people and problems, even when we see how self-defeating they are. And even after making a change, we may find it hard to stick to it for long.

Indeed, one area in which this basic human trait has been much noted recently is medical compliance. People go to doctors and are told what steps are necessary to treat their physical ailments. Patients are given regimes of drugs and are told to make certain changes in exercise, diet, and various other things. Yet the extent of noncompliance with such doctor's orders is truly staggering. Studies suggest that no more than half of patients keep to long-term treatments. Even with short-term ones, many miss taking pills and disregard warnings about diet and over-exertion. Some do not take their medicine at all. Thus we find this resistance to changes in routine even in the crucial realm of physical health.

This same human trait may also prevent one thoroughly learning, practising and successfully applying the coping tech-niques covered in earlier chapters. One may be blocked from making the necessary changes for a number of different reasons. These include believing the methods will not work in one's own case, not persisting long enough with them, and not making the effort required to turn them from verbal knowledge into well-practised skills. In the first half of this chapter, we look at some such common barriers to change and suggest some possible ways to overcome them.

The second half describes some "self-control" techniques developed by behavior-modification experts. These have been successfully applied to changing a variety of different behaviors, from reducing negative ones like overeating, smoking and repetitive ones such as tics to instilling positive ones like good study habits or social skills. One can use them to ensure learning and maintenance of the coping methods. In addition, they are themselves useful coping techniques.

SOME COMMON BARRIERS TO CHANGE

Seven major ones are considered here. The ideas in this section are mostly distilled from the thinking of many in the behavior-change industry; notably Jerome Frank, Victor Raimy, and Kirschenbaum and Tomarken (1982).

THE METHODS WILL NOT WORK FOR ME   This can be called resistance. It is a negative set, one which may arise for a number of different reasons. The first is no faith in the efforts of psychologists (or anyone else) to come up with coping techniques that really do work. The answer to this objection is that the methods do work; many people have found them of value.

A second reason is the belief that personal change of any sort is very slow and difficult; that one's ways can only be altered by tortuous, extended effort and that even these coping techniques will make little real difference. Once again, the answer to this is that people do make radical shifts in their ways of thinking and lifestyles overnight. People may become converts after a single encounter with a charismatic exponent of an ideology or religion, for example. Some people, even without aid, manage to give up such dearly held habits as smoking and drinking.

A third reason is a mistaken belief in one's own incompetence. One may say "Yes, these methods may work for others but not for me, because I am destined to be a failure". As we saw earlier, one can build up a negative self-image through a long history of failure or some greater vulnerability to stress than others, due to traumatic early experiences or genetic makeup. And we saw how this belief can lead to that deadly enemy of

176

effective coping, a sense of helplessness, isolation and general demoralization. With such a negative view, one may either give up very easily or not try at all.

A possible way through this barrier is simply to experiment. Try the methods and see if they work for you. Whether they will or will not is a hypothesis open to test. One psychologist raises the analogy of being in a clothing shop. A clerk may show an item which at the moment seems to be the wrong color and style but he says "Try it on for size and see. You might like it."

Trying and finding out may lead to a few early experiences of success which should do much to combat demoralization and a negative self-image. You can see that the success really is due to your own actions, that you have learned skills that really work. This should also give motivation to keep trying.

HAVING A POOR BUT STABLE ADJUSTMENT   As described in Chapter 1, we may reach some sort of more-or-less stable adjustment to our circumstances. Sometimes it is not the best possible, however. For instance, the highly gifted child who finds school dull may withdraw into himself, or an agoraphobic may cope with fear of outside events by staying at home all the time.

People may indeed become very adept at protecting themselves in various ways. Thus a poor adjustment which buys some peace may date back many years and be very resistant to alteration. It may also be the only one that a person knows.

A counter to this difficulty is to develop a new perspective on one's own ways. The aim of Part 1 of this book was to give such a new way of thinking about and understanding how people do cope and adapt, as an aid to identifying and understanding one's own characteristics.

The major difficulty here is that many of us have little insight into our own behavior, even when very perceptive about others'. A Buddhist saying expresses this idea well, "The eye sees but cannot see itself". And if a defence mechanism like denial is operating at full throttle even an eye that can turn inward may as well be blind.

A possible solution is to seek advice and feedback from others for self-understanding. Generally, we do not get a great deal of this in normal social life, tact and diplomacy being essential survival skills. While such feedback may hurt at first, in the long run it can be very useful.

NOT TAKING EMOTIONAL RISKS Many actions necessary to meet our needs and ensure a good adjustment require taking a few emotional risks. We risk rejection upon asking for a date, expressing love, offering friendship or proposing marriage, for example. Other actions can invite aggression or retaliation. Examples are requesting a raise, taking someone to task for some highly annoying faults, or getting an inevitable confrontation over with. Shifts in job or residence involve the risk of temporary social isolation.

Trying out the techniques covered in earlier chapters also can be an emotional risk. For example, one may wish to test one's powers to withstand provocation in a particularly difficult situation by using relaxation or stress-inoculation techniques.

Many people are unduly frightened by the chance of failure, so much so that they take few emotional risks. As a result, little positive coping action may be made and much missed out on. Needs do not get met, situations which might be resolved with a little pain are not. In this situation Albert Ellis's RET method of thinking through the consequences of failing, of suffering a little emotional pain, is of use. This was described in Chapter 10. Ask, "What will happen if I fail, if I am rejected? Will it be so awful that I will physically wither up and die or will it just pass after a day or so? Will I never live it down?" Looking at the other side of this coin may also help. Ask what will happen if you do not try at all, if you continue on as at present. Will that be worse than running some risks now, suffering some inevitable failures but perhaps eventually succeeding?

OTHERS SHOULD CHANGE INSTEAD, THEY MUST TREAT ME BETTER Albert Ellis puts this forward as another irrational idea that can lead to faulty adjustment. It is like an ideological block. One sees one's own ways and habits as more or less the correct ones, which others should conform to. One has a presently high level of stress because things are not as they should be. This particular notion may be the explanation for some migrants never adapting to a new culture. They still see their ways as right and refuse to accommodate to those of their host society.

One counter is simply to be more pragmatic. Yes, there often are many things that others do that they should not. Yes, our rights are sometimes neglected or trampled on. People and events are often not as they should be. But, satisfactory adjusting means accommodating to the way the world is rather than how one would like it to be. Often we must swallow much that is unpalatable.

GIVING UP TOO SOON   One result of feeling demoralized and inadequate can be to give up early. Some early failures or lack of progress just confirm a negative self-image. One expected to fail and did. Yet it is very important to persist. As mentioned, the techniques may take time to learn and practise. Change can often only come about slowly, and one must force oneself to keep working no matter how painful it is at first. With a few successes a sense of mastery may begin to develop.

Persistence can be enhanced by enlisting the aid of others to keep you motivated. It is very hard to keep to any change programme if you have to supply all the energy yourself. Others can praise your successes and help you through the unavoidable failures. Another aid to persistence is programming some rewards for small changes, rewards other than the intrinsic one of seeing positive results. We look at this in more detail in the next section.

A very common reason for not persisting at a change programme is a single relapse. A smoker trying to quit may suddenly crack one day and light up, even after months of valiant abstinence. A dieter might break down one night and go on a binge after weeks of admirable restraint. Or, after mastering some stress-inoculation techniques to handle anger or anxiety, one may find one just cannot successfully bring them to bear in a particular situation. Such relapses often happen. Few people seem to be immune. Unfortunately, having once cracked, a person may totally abandon the change regime and go right back to old ways.

Marlatt and Gordon (1980) have suggested how this process might take place. First, a person encounters a "high-risk" situation. It could be one in which he or she has great difficulty withstanding anxiety or anger, or one with strong interpersonal conflict, or one where a reformed drinker or smoker faces much social or internal pressure to crack. And he or she either makes no active coping response or just a very weak one and so "fails". As a result of this failure, he or she capitulates and reverts to old ways. Beck's thinking error of overgeneralization seems to operate here, a person overgeneralizing from one lapse to a feeling of complete failure. It may batter the image of self-efficacy built up through earlier efforts.

A number of responses are possible here. One is simply not to overgeneralize. See a relapse as it is, just as a brief break and resolve to go right back to trying again. Another is to avoid high-risk situations. Work out what they are for you and treat them like the bubonic plague. Also recall that one has learned skills, not magical panaceas. Sometimes skills are not applied or are not up to handling given circumstances.

HAVING NEGATIVE SETS Just as Marvin had one to be depressed, a person may have a negative one to resist change. Hopefully the perspective promoted in earlier chapters will help identify and provide steps to remedy this. An adaptive set to try to replace them with is the positive problem-solving one, like that of the Mercury astronauts mentioned in Chapter 6.

FLAK FROM OTHERS FOR CHANGING People around us eventually get used to the way that we are. To them, we may acquire a certain predictability which they may find reassuring. As well, some traits or ways we have (which we dislike) they may greatly like. For example, a wife may feel secure with her hen-pecked husband's timidity. Indeed, people can gain a vested interest in keeping us the way we are. So, when we do change in a positive direction, they may provide much flak and resistance to it. That social pressure thus may be a strong check to further growth. Unfortunately, it is one that is hard to suggest effective general ways to deal with.

An apocryphal story along these lines concerns a young man who had a drug problem. His girlfriend felt that he was destroying himself and continually harangued him to stop. This went on for months until he finally heeded her warnings and did quit. They broke off their relationship very soon after this change. She had really liked him the way he was, feeling that her constant admonitions gave her an important role. When that was taken away, there was not much else left, and so she went in search of a relationship that would allow her to adopt this role again.

SOME SELF-CONTROL TECHNIQUES

Many of us at some time take up a new interest with great enthusiasm and zeal. We may start a new course in a foreign language, in classical dancing or art appreciation. We may set out on a regular exercise, diet or yoga programme, or one to cut down on our excessive smoking or coffee drinking. But after a few weeks or months the interest somehow begins to wane, the exercise, work or class attendance rate plummets, and finally one sinks back into old habits. Yet while this is the fate of many, there are others who succeed. They give up a bad habit permanently, keep to an exercise programme for years, and finish their course of study. Why do some succeed where many fail?

The everyday explanation is usually "willpower", an elusive trait that some lucky people have but others do not. Many are thought to fail because they have the right intentions but not the willpower to stay the course. Fortunately this explanation is not really correct. What appears to be iron will in others is often just their knowledge of a few basic self-control techniques. They organize themselves and their lives to maximize the chances of success. Behavior modifiers have come up with a set which can be applied to a variety of different situations. One can use them to banish self-defeating, maladaptive behaviors, and help instill more positive behaviors, such as building a strong social network, learning and practising coping techniques, and keeping to an exercise or study programme.

MAKE A CONTRACT TO CHANGE   This may well be the most important. Before setting out on a behavior-change programme of any sort, make a commitment to persist that will make you think very hard before deciding to quit. This commitment could actually be a written contract. It could set out exactly what you have to do (exercise for thirty minutes every second day, lose one kilogram a week) and prescribe what will happen if you do not. The penalty can be as dire and draconian as you wish. You could give something valuable to a friend with strict instructions to keep or sell it if you deviate from the straight and narrow. Many weight-watcher groups use this idea. They relieve their raw recruits of a large sum of money at the start which is not given back unless they finish the programme.

RECORD YOUR PROGRESS   Keeping a record of the

frequency of a behavior you are trying to modify, or of your efforts to combat it, is usually helpful. For example, you can tally the number of cigarettes smoked each day, the number of weekly exercise sessions, number of weekly relaxation-training sessions, or amount of time spent working productively at something. This record can tell you how well (or how badly) you are progressing, and thus when you need to put in extra effort. Signs of progress are also a good spur to keep at your programme. Sometimes the very act of taking a record can create much change in behavior. One can be truly astounded by just how frequent a certain behavior is.

As well, a record can often make clear the circumstances which induce certain behaviors. Much of what we do is spurred on by certain cues, certain situations. Smoking might be more likely when a person is bored or anxious, fighting with a spouse more likely at mealtimes, or overeating when watching television late at night. A student may get little study done because he tries to work in a place with many distractions. If you know what situations spark off a certain habit, you can minimize its frequency by avoiding them. By the same token, if you know the circumstances that favor positive behaviors you can make them more likely.

REWARD YOURSELF FOR CHANGE   Much of what we do is aimed at getting certain rewards and avoiding punishments. One reason why some habits are hard to break is that the rewards for them are often immediate and strong, while the ones for breaking them, even though more powerful, are located in the distant future. Overeating is a good example. Food is an instant reward while the reward of restraint is far off; better health and looking and feeling much better. Immediate rewards usually exert more force. The same thing happens with instilling positive behaviors like more exercise. Again, the rewards may not show up for many weeks, and a person may suffer numerous aches and pains before then.

Such a lean supply of immediate rewards is often why people take a long time to begin a really big task, like painting the house, hunting for a new job or even writing a book. We often only reward ourselves for finishing the whole project, only then getting a sense of accomplishment. Since that reward is far off, we may find it hard to start and persist. One solution is to break a large task into smaller, component ones, and pat yourself on the back for completing each part.

An author trying to start his first book once used this method. He had never really been able to settle down to write, dithering for hours after grinding out a few words. He would gaze out the window and be distracted by just about anything. Eventually he told himself to think of the book not as one four-hundred-page tome but as eighteen separate chapters, each chapter being one single unit. One big task became eighteen small ones, each of which he would reward himself for finishing.

Punishment can also be self-applied. You can punish yourself for a too-high rate of maladaptive behaviors or a too-low rate of positive ones. A man having frequent arguments with his wife once applied this principle. Every time they fought he made himself sit for a certain period on a stool in the garage, a far from exciting prospect. That was enough to dramatically cut down the frequency of the arguments. A student trying to write a thesis used it to get himself to work. He gave an acquaintance numerous cheques made out to organizations that he really loathed, such as the Ku Klux Klan and American Nazi Party. Every time he failed to write a specified number of pages in a week, his friend posted one of the cheques, a severe punishment indeed. That added spur was enough.

RESIST WHEN TEMPTATION IS STILL FAR OFF The idea behind this principle is to decide to resist a maladaptive behavior when that is still an easy decision to make. Catch yourself early in the chain of events and exert your will then. For example, let us say you often overspend while shopping and cannot really afford to. Before going out make a list of what you actually need and only take enough money to cover it. And leave the credit cards at home.

If possible, physically prevent an undesired behavior from occurring. The hero Ulysses used this method, in a tale from Greek mythology. His ship once had to pass by the Sirens, three beautiful sea-nymphs whose magnificent singing lured ships to destruction on their rocky island. Ulysses wanted to hear their voices without also having to suffer the usual dire consequence; being eaten. So while still out of earshot and able to resist, he stuffed his crewmen's ears with wax and had himself firmly tied to the mast. The crew was given strict instructions not to release him until they were well past the witches. Thus, even if he changed his mind and wanted to jump over the side, he could not.

The famous French author Victor Hugo used this method to instill a positive behavior; working. In the morning he figured out the hour at which he would finish his daily quota of pages. His servant then took away all his clothes and did not return them until the appointed time, so Hugo could not leave even if he wanted to. Thus there was nothing else to do but work.

Fighting temptation when it is easy is also recommended for that sort of person who continually wants to test his or her strength and resolve. For example, an errant husband might spend time in the apartments of secretaries or a dieter stroll down streets full of bakeries and delicatessens. Generally, such a policy turns out not to be sound.

USE CUE STRENGTHENING This is a method for making particular behaviors more likely in certain situations. The idea behind it is simple. Certain cues spark off certain behaviors. So, perform a certain action only in a particular situation, so it then becomes a stronger cue for that action. Stuart and Davis teach their weight-reducing clients to only eat in one room; never in any others in their house. Thus that room becomes a cue for eating, and a person will be more likely not to eat if he or she stays out of it. A student trying to study better should make a desk situation a cue for study and nothing else; not daydreaming, reading novels and so on. So, he or she should only study at that desk, and do nothing else there. That way the desk situation will set the occasion for study and study alone.

This method is also sometimes used in treating insomnia. One factor that increases the trouble insomniacs have in getting to sleep is that their bedroom becomes the cue for many behaviors other than sleeping. They eat, watch television, and do all kinds of interesting puzzles and games. As well, if a person cannot sleep and tosses and turns for hours, the bedroom can become a cue for tossing and turning rather than falling asleep. The recommended technique is to strengthen the bedroom as a cue for sleeping and nothing else. Insomniacs are instructed to do nothing but sleep there and toss out all games, television sets and so on. If they are not able to fall asleep after about twenty minutes, they are told to go to another room and do something else, only to return when actually feeling sleepy.

BE SPECIFIC ABOUT WHAT MUST CHANGE   Finally, when applying self-monitoring and reward techniques, make sure that you specify exactly what must change. Make it clear what behaviors must be altered, and make sure they are measurable. Otherwise the behaviors are much more difficult to modify. For example, if you wish to study more, break down this aim into highly specific tasks. These might be: read one chapter of book X each day, spend one hour a day examining and revising lecture notes, write ten pages of assignments this weekend.

CHAPTER 13

Psychotherapy: Advanced/Remedial Training in Coping

Sometimes one's problems in living, in coping with and adapting to stressful circumstances, can seem insurmountable. While most of us usually weather our life crises somehow, at times many still falter. The stressors look overwhelming and one's confidence in being able to deal with them sinks to a low ebb. One may feel what Jerome Frank (1976) calls "demoralization", impotence and helplessness in the face of events, a sense of aloneness and isolation. It is nearly the opposite of that attitude of self-efficacy that seems to make for good coping. According to Frank, the more demoralized a person is, the worse his or her symptoms (such as anxiety, depression, and strength of defensive manoeuvres) become. There appears to be no clear path through a maze of difficulties, no certain way to proceed.

One answer to this syndrome is psychotherapy, defined here as personal help from an expert on problems in living. All of us have at some time been helped by a relative, friend or counsellor to get through a crisis, to get information at a critical life junction or to guide us through some problems for which we have no useful solutions. Psychotherapy is a couple of steps beyond such neighborliness.

It may promote one's capacity to cope in several ways. First, as Marvin Goldfried has argued, psychotherapy can be seen essentially as training in coping skills. It can give a person the confidence and the necessary new knowledge to better deal with life. It can give a person a clear idea of just what his or her particular difficulties are and how best to tackle them. As mentioned earlier, often we have little insight into our own behavior and a good therapist can serve as an excellent mirror to show us. One's most deep-seated irrational ideas, conflicts or maladaptive thinking styles may be pointed out. One can both gain self-understanding and try out new ways of behaving in a comfortable, accepting and supportive atmosphere. As well, just talking to a sympathetic listener can be a great boon, relieving the feelings of mental distress, of maladjustment. One can gain new perspectives on oneself, and the ways one relates to others.

Who actually seeks psychotherapy? What sorts of maladjustments do they normally suffer from? Frank (1976) categorizes typical consumers. Three of his categories are as follows. First is the *shaken*, people temporarily demoralized and unable to cope with their immediate life situation. They may be suffering a brief crisis such as divorce or diagnosis of a major illness, and in part just need reassurance. Another category is *neurotics*, people who have learned very maladaptive ways of dealing with stress early in life (for example obsessive-compulsive neurosis) and whose normal development as persons has been arrested as a result. Third is the *discontented*, the hordes now struggling with our society's major problems; crises of identity, feelings of alienation, of existential despair. They see their lives as lacking meaning and purpose.

Some more characteristics of psychotherapy clients are given by Weiner (1975). Most common, he says, is the person conscious of mental pain which he or she seeks to have relieved. Anxiety and depression with no obvious cause are two examples. Others go because their friends go; it is currently the "in" thing to do. Some go for a very human reason indeed; to get a clean bill of psychological health. This bill they can present to spouse or family members, thus laying the blame for particular difficulties at a sparring partner's feet. And some go to improve their already fruitful and rewarding lives even further, to gain new skills to make their lives better.

Most clients bring with them a set of hopes and fears about therapy, also listed by Weiner (1975). Most hope to feel better right away, and to rapidly improve thereafter. They expect to talk a lot about themselves. A variety of fears may be there; to have one's independence undermined, to be instantly hospitalized as "crazy", and to learn terrible things about oneself.

And what about the psychotherapist who is to help combat these problems and satisfy the above hopes? He or she may come from one of several backgrounds. At the top of the prestige and remuneration totem pole are psychiatrists, who have a medical degree plus advanced training in psychotherapy. Many of these tend to favor more medically oriented treatments, prescribing drugs and seeing many emotional disturbances as not unlike physical diseases. Some even believe that most emotional disorders have a clear biological basis, which eventually will be found.

A psychologist is not medically trained, having instead a degree from a university psychology department. They tend to see emotional problems as due more to faulty learning or thinking. They also usually have training in the administration of psychological tests, which analyze basic personality traits, mental abilities and so on. A psychiatric nurse either has a degree in nursing or has hospital training, with further experience in a psychiatric ward.

But anyone from virtually any background may call himself a psychotherapist and conduct psychotherapy. And many do, especially exponents of the less established therapies, like bioenergetics and encounter groups. Indeed, studies suggest that the therapist's background is much less important than his or her personality. Certain traits make a good therapist. High on the list are personal warmth, sincerity and genuineness. He or she should be able to provide a warm, accepting atmosphere and be someone the client can trust, respect and like. The therapist should also have good interpersonal skills, and a good sense of empathy. Inevitably, some are better than others. Some do their best work with certain sorts of problems or types of patient. They should tell you this. And, as in every profession, some are hacks who may do more harm than good.

Just as good therapists have certain qualities, so do the clients most likely to be helped. These are not hard and fast rules however, just indicators of a likely good result. Weiner (1975) lists a few. First, not too surprisingly, it is better if the client is quite verbal. This just means being adept at verbalizing thoughts, feelings and problems and being able to readily understand and learn from the therapist's suggestions. Second, it helps if the client is likeable (therapists are also human) and wants to change. And the client will be more likely to benefit if he or she has a history of sustained effort of trying to change.

What should the client expect to happen? First, he or she should expect a very close relationship to develop. In the first few sessions, the therapist may just mostly listen. He or she will try to understand what the client's particular difficulty is. He or she should then say what the goals of treatment will be, exactly what will be done and why, and how long it should all take. Different therapies diverge here. Classical psychoanalysis can take years, and others only a single or a handful of sessions. Usually the two draw up a contract, specifying what their goals are, what each is expected to do (for example, attend regularly, and so on) and agree to the treatment. They then proceed to do just that until either one feels the time has come to end the relationship, for whatever reason.

While all psychotherapies have some features in common, there are many different types. Therapists are supposed to become more alike in what they do (with experience) but they begin with quite different theories and techniques. They belong to different schools of thought. Coleman, Butcher and Carson (1980) slice up these differences into some categories. First is length — some therapies take years, others much less. Most nowadays take between six and ten sessions. Some have a "here and now" focus, being concerned with what the client is thinking, feeling and doing in the present. Others probe back into the past, especially looking at childhood experiences. Some are very directive. An example is Albert Ellis's rational–emotive therapy in which the client's irrational ideas are repeatedly attacked. Others, like client-centred therapy, are just the opposite: All the therapist does is provide an accepting atmosphere in which the client tries to work out his problems himself.

The goals (and language in which ideas are expressed) of the therapies differ. Most goals of most therapies fit the following list given by Coleman *et al.* The first goal is to change maladaptive behavior, such as eating or drinking too much, having bitter marital quarrels, and so on. Second is improving interpersonal skills. These include the social skills examined in Chapter 5 and ones such as good communication and relationship skills. Third is to resolve inner conflicts and lessen the mental distress that brings

189

so many to therapy in the first place. Fourth is to change faulty ideas about oneself and the world. Some of these we saw in Chapter 10, but there are many others in just about every sphere in life. Very common ones are about sex. People can learn some very strange ideas about sex indeed, which may place great strains upon a relationship or marriage.

Fifth is to foster a sense of identity, to let a person find out who he or she is. Sixth is minimizing purely environmental causes of maladaptive behavior. These may be obscure to the client but crystal clear to the therapist. For example, the therapist may see that a client only overeats when watching television on lonely nights or that he only fights with his wife at mealtimes. Thus the therapist can instruct the client on what steps to take to minimize such environmental causes of behavior.

Let us now turn to some of the major psychotherapies. Behind each is a theory of the mind and specific therapeutic techniques. The list is far from exhaustive because there are literally hundreds of different types of therapy. It is meant only as a survey and brief description of some major ones. The book by Coleman *et al.* is ideal further reading.

PSYCHOANALYSIS

Many people believe psychotherapy and psychoanalysis to be the same thing. But this is not at all so. Psychoanalysis is a particular method of therapy, one that rests largely upon the teachings of Sigmund Freud. He developed a complex theory of the human mind based in large part on his keen observations of Viennese patients around the turn of the century. The method is usually the longest, the most expensive, and the most controversial because there is little really hard evidence that it works.

A psychoanalytic therapist is usually a psychiatrist (and only rarely a psychologist) with additional advanced training at a psychoanalytic institute. The therapist himself is psychoanalyzed there, a process taking a year or longer, by an experienced initiate.

The theory has the human mind divided into three parts. The *id* is the storehouse of all our basic drives: hunger, thirst, sex

190

and so on. A newborn baby is almost pure id; it has drives and sets about meeting them with no regard for anyone or anything else. The *ego* is the "I" which develops over time. Essentially it tries to regulate, to divert the id's drives into socially acceptable channels. It contains all the defence mechanisms that we looked at in Chapter 2. Finally, the *superego* develops last of all. It is like a conscience, a moral structure watching with a stern eye over the id and ego. These three parts to the mind are constantly doing battle with each other. Just like Western European nations of the past, their interests conflict and must somehow be resolved. Freud felt that many emotional disorders were due to deep conflicts between the three, conflicts which were repressed because the individual could not face them.

Psychoanalytic therapy often aims at a total reconstruction of the personality, no mean feat. The therapist tries to give the patient insight into his unconscious conflicts and the way his ego is trying to deal with particular id impulses. The therapist aims at replacing the ego's old, maladaptive defensive manoeuvres with more healthy, adaptive ones.

To this end, Coleman *et al.* describe four major techniques used. Perhaps the most popular is free-association. Here the client sits comfortably and has to say whatever comes to mind, be they thoughts, feelings, associations, opinions or whatever. The therapist interprets these, seeing them as expressions of deep conflicts and motives which would not come out in normal speech. Another method is dream interpretation. Freud called dreams the "royal road to the unconscious". The therapist looks for certain recurring themes in them, since conflicts may be expressed in disguised form within a dream.

Psychoanalysts also use a close analysis of two very real phenomena in psychotherapy; resistance and transference. Resistance is a client's unwillingness or even inability to talk about certain feelings or events. He or she may, for instance, steer the conversation away from any talk of parents. The therapist may use this as a way of understanding the client, asking the question of why resistance in specific areas is occurring.

Transference often takes place when the therapy relationship deepens. The client may transfer to the therapist feelings he or she had to someone important in his life. He may, for example, react to the therapist with some of the hostility, anger and ambivalence he felt toward his father. Coleman *et al.* point out that the therapist may use this therapeutically, giving the client the experience of having a "good" father so he may work through his feelings.

Classical psychoanalysis is not all that common nowadays. But a shorter variant of the method, often called psychodynamic therapy, is quite popular.

HUMANISTIC THERAPIES

These usually rest on a somewhat different notion of what the human mind is all about and what can go wrong. The basic idea is that people are free to make choices, to think about and understand their problems, and to act to solve them: The therapist is more a guide than anything else (Coleman *et al.* 1980). These ideas have filtered through to many areas in our society, industrial management and teaching being two notable examples. Here we look at three of the many therapies based on this approach.

CLIENT-CENTRED THERAPY This one goes back to the 1940s where a psychologist named Carl Rogers put it together. It is very non-directive. The therapist tries hard not to force his ideas upon the client, or even to greatly interpret what he or she says. There is no real probe for deeper meanings, for early traumatic experiences, no suggestions as to what solutions the client might try. The therapist aims only to provide a warm, accepting relationship; to listen to and perhaps more clearly restate what the client is saying. The theory is that within this atmosphere of unconditional positive regard and respect, clients can find their own path back to sound adjustment. Coleman *et al.* say that the pure form of this therapy is rare today, but Rogers' ideas still enjoy much influence.

GESTALT THERAPY The word gestalt means *whole*, and the basic idea behind this therapy is to make the mind and body whole. The therapist tries to make a person more self-aware and self-accepting, to put the mind in touch with the body and what it is feeling. Often the therapy takes place in a group, the therapist focusing on particular individuals in it in succession.

Some of Gestalt therapy's ideas were borrowed from psychoanalysis. A person is thought to have unresolved conflicts and early traumas not worked through which are carried into new relationships. Practitioners have renamed them "unfinished business". Individuals by various means are brought to a point where they must confront this unfinished business and hopefully eliminate its future influence.

Gestalt therapists use a variety of different techniques. They may look at dreams, or to better get a person in touch with feelings ask him or her to "be" something, and describe how it feels; to be a "tree", a "mountain", or something similar. Also popular is the empty-chair technique. A person may imagine a parent or spouse in the chair and talk to him or her, giving expression to hidden or unrelieved feelings. The therapist may get the client to switch roles, between himself and whomever is in the chair. I once saw a therapist use this method with a very mild-mannered man trying to become more assertive. He was asked to put his shyness into the chair and express his feelings toward it. This he quickly did, with an extremely colorful stream of obscenities and sheer, naked hatred.

TRANSACTIONAL ANALYSIS (TA) This is a simple scheme for looking at human interactions. It was devised by psychiatrist Eric Berne and described in his book *Games People Play* and in more detail later in Thomas Harris's *I'm O.K., You're O.K.* It is a kind of simplified and reconceived psychoanalysis.

Berne saw personality as having three ego states, which he named parent, adult and child. These are not unlike Freud's superego, ego, and id. At any time when interacting with another, he says, we are communicating through one of these three ego states. The child state is playful, and id-like in that it wants things and directly acts to get them. The adult state is ego-like, is rational, aware of social and other limits on what the person can do. The parent is superego-like, stern and commanding (for example, smoking is bad for you, you must work harder). People may tend to use one ego state more often than others, or may switch rapidly between them while talking to the same person.

As long as interactions are *uncrossed*, they go smoothly. For example, as long as person A communicates to person B as parent and B replies as child, or adult communicates to adult, all goes well. Problems arise when one person communicates as say parent, and the other replies as adult. That is a crossed interaction.

Interactions also sometimes take stereotyped forms, called *games*. Unlike scrabble and monopoly, however, they are often destructive and not fun at all. One common game is "wooden leg", where one person plays helpless because of some handicap, be it physical or social or something entirely imagined. The individual says "What do you expect from a person with such a defect". The reward for playing the helpless child is sympathy and being excused from many responsibilities. Another is "rescue", where a person takes a helpless posture, inviting certain others to come to his or her aid.

How does therapy with transactional analysis proceed? The therapist looks at a person's (or couples') characteristic ego states and games, his ways of interacting with others. Many problems may be due to faulty interaction styles, and these are pointed out to the client.

BEHAVIORAL AND COGNITIVE THERAPIES

These came from a different source than did psychoanalysis and the humanistic therapies. The basic ideas came from experimental psychology; from psychologists studying learning, memory, perception and thinking.

Behavioral therapists see maladaptive behavior not so much as the product of deep inner conflicts, which need to be resolved by a client gaining insight into them, but as arising from faulty learning. For example, while a psychoanalyst might see overeating or some sexual problems as due to such conflicts, a behavioral therapist might see them as due to faulty environmental control or faulty learning. Rather than striving to give the client "insight", he would directly work on the behavior itself. Other difficulties would be seen as due to a client not learning certain skills, certain behaviors. So therapy consists of teaching and reinforcing them.

We can briefly illustrate the behavioral therapists' approach with a classic textbook case; that of a man with an extreme fetish for prams. These objects for some reason caused him great excitement. He could not, for example, have satisfactory sex with his wife without visualizing prams. His behavior therapist saw this problem as an instance of classical conditioning, prams serving as a conditioned stimulus eliciting sexual excitement. So, he set out to replace one conditioned response with another. A classical conditioning procedure was implemented in which prams were associated with induced nausea over a course of therapy sessions. Eventually they came to make the patient sick rather than lustful, and he was pronounced "cured".

Behavioral therapists use a wide variety of techniques. Indeed, many of the ones described in this book are taken from this basic approach; techniques ranging from systematic desensitization and flooding to social-skills training.

Cognitive therapists look at the influence of faulty thinking on behavior. They see much maladaptive behavior, many emotional problems, as due to irrational thoughts or erroneous thinking styles. We saw this approach in Chapter 10, Ellis's rational–emotive therapy and Beck's cognitive therapy being described in some detail. Therapy consists of identifying a client's habitual thinking styles and errors and then perhaps conducting a Socratic dialogue to try to get him or her to abandon them. The many techniques described in Chapter 10 may be used to achieve such a change.

DO THE THERAPIES WORK?

This is still a crucial question. And if they do work, just how effective are they?

An early answer was given by British psychologist Hans Eysenck in 1952. He argued that psychotherapy does not work at all, since while about two-thirds of clients exposed to it recover within two years or so, so does the same proportion without it. Not surprisingly, this conclusion caused a storm of protest and spawned a series of studies to try to decide the question for certain.

Bergin and Lamber (1978) suggest that psychotherapy can speed up improvement that would have occurred anyway, and ensure in some cases changes in maladaptive behavior that would not have taken place without therapy. However, two very recent works have suggested a quite different conclusion. Zilbergeld (1983) argues that while behavior therapy may be useful in special circumstances (such as in dealing with a highly specific problem like a phobia), most therapies that involve just client–therapist talking have little or no real effect. Prioleau, Murdock and Brody (1983) reviewed a large number of studies which compared psychotherapy (excluding behavior therapy) with placebo treatment. (A placebo is an agent that has no inherent effect itself, but which may create one if a person believes strongly that it will. People often recover from a variety of conditions after taking a course of sugar pills, for example, if they are convinced that the pills are really some potent drug.) These authors concluded that psychotherapy had no greater effect than a placebo.

But one cannot regard the question as settled. Evaluating how well psychotherapy works is a very tricky business at any time. Different therapists have different goals and thus quite divergent ideas about what constitutes success. A behavior therapist may aim for a specific change in some behavior while a Gestalt therapist simply intends to make a client aware of various choices. As well, a whole range of subtle effects may occur that an evaluation study just does not detect. And finally, as in any profession, some practitioners may do more harm than good, cancelling out, in a survey, the positive benefits effected by good therapists. Many people have indeed reported that therapy greatly improved their lives, and such evidence has to be taken seriously.

CHAPTER 14

Summing Up

This book had two major aims. The first was to give some broad overview of the general problem of adjustment to circumstances and managing the stress that a poor fit between person and environment can cause. The goal was to give a perspective, a vantage point from which to examine this critical topic. To this end, we examined the stress reaction and the evolutionary reasons why we experience it. We looked at some major ways people use to cope with stressors, noting that these fell into two major classes; direct-action methods and palliatives. Chapter 3 examined some major stressors, emphasizing the ones that most of us are eventually likely to face. Chapter 4 examined coping with extreme stressors and Chapter 5 the role of social factors in reducing (and in sometimes causing) much of the stress of life. The final chapter in Part 1 tried to find some reasons for the wide individual differences that occur in response to stress. That chapter also suggested that an important aspect to coping effectively was a positive mental attitude; a sense of mastery, of self-efficacy.

Part 2 examined some major stress management techniques. Chapter 7 briefly described how physical factors like diet and exercise could enhance one's power to cope effectively. Chapter 9 detailed how prior experiences of stress could help inoculate a person against later ones. Chapter 10 elaborated on the role of faulty thinking, of erroneous appraisal, on adjustment. It pointed out that thinking which is too out of line with reality can turn innocuous events into stressors, and, because a person's model of how things work is awry, lead to more stress. Finally, Chapter 12 looked at some barriers to change, which also are blocks against finding a better adjustment.

The wealth of facts, theories and phenomena described in

the course of creating this perspective hopefully will allow the reader to better understand his or her own difficulties, for at least two reasons. The first is by realizing that often there is little unique about one's own problems in coping, that many people have quite similar ones for more or less the same reasons. The second is simply through becoming aware of some typical stressors, a few barriers to sound adjustment, and how the faulty ways in which one copes with stress may ultimately be the cause of much more of it.

The overall aim of Part 2 of this book was to offer a menu, a set of techniques to help a person under stress find answers to the questions "What can I do about it?" and "How can I stop this much stress occurring in the future?" Learning, practising and trying out the methods listed may with time convert them from just techniques to a set of coping skills. As with skills such as driving or playing tennis well, they may become automatic. One may then learn to anticipate and counter imminent stressors, without having to think too much about the process. But again, Part 2 is a menu rather than a prescription. It is important to select out the items from it that best suit you.

And finally, much of the material in this book suggests that many problems in adjustment are due to humanity living in environments different from those we evolved to cope with. The most striking instance is the stress reaction itself. As described in Chapter 1, this response is too often counterproductive rather than adaptive in modern life. Another instance is described in Chapter 7. Though humanity is meant to be physically active, the usual city environment and lifestyle greatly predisposes people to be sedentary instead. A third case is the social world. Some ethologists have argued that we evolved to live in relatively small groups in which each member knows all others well, and in which kinship ties are very important. Again, the typical large-city environment is very far from such an ideal, which may be one cause of the pervasive loneliness, alienation and bizarre behaviors so often seen there.

We can now turn to a couple of summaries of some other writers' advice for a less stressful, better adjusted life. Since these are drawn from much the same body of research, their suggestions overlap to some extent with those of the present book.

One prescription was put forward by Hans Selye, one of the best-known researchers on stress. His work has been mentioned in a number of places already. The list of suggestions given here comes from what he calls the "scientifically verifiable laws that govern the body's reactions in . . . living in satisfying equilibrium with its surroundings" (Selye, 1980). He advises a number of things.

First is to "find your own natural predilections and stress level". As discussed in Chapter 6, people differ greatly on many factors such as abilities, stress tolerance, preferences, and so on. Selye suggests self-analysis to determine just what one needs and wants in life, and how much work one is prepared to do to achieve one's aims. Find your optimum level of stress and try to keep within narrow limits around it, whenever possible. This advice requires a firm idea of one's abilities and capacity for work.

Second is to "practise altruistic egoism". This point derives from one of Selye's basic ideas about the nature of human beings and indeed all thinking life; a belief of all organisms in the primary importance of oneself. He advises us to consider ourselves a great deal (though also others) and store up the goodwill, esteem and social support of our fellows. To put this another way, store up social resources for a rainy day.

Selye (1980) also suggests some further general ways of dealing with stress. The first two are straightforward: do not let basically neutral, harmless events become stressors, and organize one's life well enough to bypass any genuine ones that it is not necessary to face. He then suggests consciously working at becoming adept in handling stressors that one cannot or does not want to simply avoid, and to seek relaxation and rest from the demands of life at frequent intervals. He also advises working out the difference between stress due to going beyond the limits of one's adaptive powers and "understress", resulting from too little stimulation, since the two need to be dealt with in different ways.

A somewhat longer and more detailed list of prescriptions is given by Martin Shaffer (1982). Some of his major suggestions are as follows. His view is that an essential starting point in adjustment is to "decide to live", to make a conscious decision to continue existing. This move sets the stage for gathering up the energy to go about the remaining points. Then one has to give oneself reasons for living. We saw in Chapter 4 that a major way some concentration-camp survivors got through their ordeal was by having this strong reason to survive. But this can also be important in everyday life: having good reasons to live again may aid in the struggle to get through temporary crises. The German philosopher Nietzsche summarized the idea with, "He who has a 'why' can endure any 'how'".

Shaffer also advises developing an optimistic attitude toward life and oneself. Such an attitude seems to be a part of the sense of mastery that was described in Chapter 6, a confidence that one will eventually overcome current trials and tribulations, a sense that one can handle the stressors that come one's way. Another point is to keep one's thinking flexible, considering many different ways of approaching and adjusting to new situations. "Keep an open mind" is a simple way of putting it. As we saw in Chapters 10 and 11, overly rigid thinking may result in poor adjustment to circumstances.

Shaffer also suggests trying to see stressful situations as opportunities and challenges rather than negative experiences, or catastrophes. Naturally this is not always possible, or even desirable sometimes, and will also depend on one's coping skills and resources. But it seems something worthwhile to aim for. Another suggestion is to actively participate in one's fate. This means becoming actively involved in realms of life which to you are important; work, family and leisure pursuits.

Shaffer's final suggestion is to "become responsible". Accept yourself as you are; with all your feelings, beliefs, habits and thoughts. Avoid blaming others for events that go wrong, for the way that things are. Take on the responsibility yourself.

One must understand, however, that the above list is an ideal, a model to strive toward. It seems very doubtful that any mere mortal could live up to it completely, and certainly not in every sphere of life.

This brings us to the end of our trek through the critical realm of coping and adaptation. I close with a final lesson for effective adjustment given by the great composer Richard Wagner. He described a major theme in his epic opera tetralogy *The Ring of the Nibelungs* in this way:

The entire poem sets forth the necessity of recognizing and yielding to the changeable, the many-faceted ... the eternal renewing of reality and of life ... That is the lesson that we must learn from the history of mankind — to will what necessity imposes, and, thus, ourselves, to bring it about.

Literature Cited

Adams, D. *The Restaurant at the End of the Universe*. London: Pan, 1980.

Adams, D. *Life, the Universe and Everything*. London: Pan, 1982.

Bandura, A. "Self-efficacy: Toward a Unifying Theory of Behavioral Change". *Psychological Review*, 1977, *84*, 191–215.

Beck, A. T. *Cognitive Therapy and the Emotional Disorders*. New York: International Universities Press, 1976.

Bedrosian, R. C. and Beck, A. T. "Principles of Cognitive Therapy". In M. J. Mahoney (Ed.), *Psychotherapy Process*. New York: Plenum, 1980.

Benner, P., Roskies, E. and Lazarus, R. S. "Stress and Coping under Extreme Conditions". In J. E. Dimsdale (Ed.), *Survivors, Victims, and Perpetrators*. New York: Hemisphere, 1980.

Bergin, A. E. and Lamber, M. J. "The Evaluation of Therapeutic Outcomes". In S. L. Garfield and A. E. Bergin (Eds.), *Handbook of Psychotherapy and Behavior Change*. New York: Wiley, 1978.

Berkman, L. F. and Syme, S. L. "Social Networks, Host Resistance, and Mortality: A Nine-year Followup Study of Alameda County Residents". *American Journal of Epidemiology*, 1979, *109*, 186–204.

Bernheim, H. *Hypnosis and Suggestion*. New Hyde Park, New Jersey: University Books, 1964.

Bourne, P. G. "Foreword". In C. R. Figley (Ed.), *Stress Disorders among Viet-Nam Veterans*. New York: Bruner/Mazel, 1978.

Brody, E. B. "Migration and Adaptation". In E. B. Brody (Ed.), *Behavior in New Environments*. Beverly Hills, California: Sage, 1970.

Browning, F. "Organizing Behind Bars". *Ramparts*, 1972, 40–5.

Burgess, A. W. and Holmstrom, L. L. "Coping Behavior of the Rape Victim". *American Journal of Psychiatry*, 1976, *133*, 413–8.

Burgess, A. W. and Holmstrom, L. L. "Recovery from Rape and Prior Life Stress". *Research in Nursing and Health*, 1978, *1*, 165–74.

Clayton, P. "A Study of Normal Bereavement". *American Journal of Psychiatry*, 1968, *125*, 168–78.

201

Cohen, F. and Lazarus, R. S. "Active Coping Processes, Coping Dispositions and Recovery from Surgery". *Psychosomatic Medicine*, 1973, *35*, 375–89.

Cohen, S. and Taylor, L. *Psychological Survival: The Experience of Long-term Imprisonment*. Harmondsworth: Penguin, 1972.

Coleman, J. C., Butcher, J. N. and Carson, R. C. *Abnormal Psychology and Modern Life*. Glenview, Illinois: Scott, Foresman, 1980.

Collins, W. R. F. "Nazi Mentality". *American Journal of Psychiatry*, 1945, *102*, 131–2.

Crisp, R. *Brazen Chariots*. New York: Norton, 1959.

Davidson, T. *Conjugal Crime*. New York: Hawthorn, 1978.

Dimsdale, J. E. "The Coping Behavior of Nazi Concentration Camp Survivors". *American Journal of Psychiatry*, 1974, *131*, 792–7.

Dubos, R. *Man Adapting*. New Haven: Yale University Press, 1965.

Dyer, E. D. "Parenthood as Crisis: A Re-study". In R. H. Moos (Ed.), *Human Adaptation*. Lexington: Heath, 1976.

D'Zurilla, T. J. and Nezu, A. "Social Problem Solving in Adults". In P. C. Kendall (Ed.), *Advances in Cognitive–Behavioral Research and Therapy*. New York: Academic Press, 1982.

Eaton, W. W. "Life Events, Social Supports, and Psychiatric Symptoms: A Reanalysis of the New Haven Data". *Journal of Health and Social Behavior*, 1978, *19*, 230–4.

Ellis, A. "The Basic Clinical Theory of Rational–Emotive Therapy". In A. Ellis and R. Grieger (Eds.), *Handbook of Rational–Emotive Therapy*. New York: Springer, 1977.

Ellis, H. C., Bennett, T. L., Daniel, T. G. and Rickert, E. J. *Psychology of Learning and Memory*. Monterey, California: Brooks/Cole, 1979.

Frank, J. D. "Restoration of Morale and Behavior Change". In A. Burton (Ed.), *What Makes Behavior Change Possible?* New York: Bruner/Mazel, 1976.

Folkman, S. and Lazarus, R. S. "An Analysis of Coping in a Middle-aged Sample". *Journal of Health and Social Behavior*, 1980, *21*, 219–39.

Goldfried, M. R. and Goldfried, A. P. "Cognitive Change Methods". In F. H. Kanfer and A. P. Goldstein (Eds.), *Helping People Change*. New York: Pergamon, 1975.

Goldfried, M. R. and Robins, C. "On the Facilitation of Self-efficacy". *Cognitive Therapy and Research*, 1982, *4*, 361–80.

Gottlieb, B. H. *Social Networks and Social Support*. Beverly Hills, California: Sage, 1981.

Gould, R. L. "The Phases of Adult Life: A Study in Developmental Psychology". *American Journal of Psychiatry*, 1972, *129*, 33–43.

Grinker, R. R. "'Mentally Healthy' Young Males (Homoclites)". *Archives of General Psychiatry*, 1962, *6*, 405–53.

Hamburg, D. A. D., Hamburg, B. and DeGoza, S. "Adaptive Problems and Mechanisms in Severely Burned Patients". *Psychiatry*, 1953, *16*, 1–20.

Havighurst, R. J. *Developmental Tasks and Education*. New York: McKay, 1972.

Hinkle, L. E. "The Effect of Exposure to Culture Change, Social Change and Changes in Interpersonal Relationships on Health". In B. S. Dohrenwend and B. P. Dohrenwend (Eds.), *Stressful Life Events*. New York: Wiley, 1973.

Hinton, J. *Dying*. Harmondsworth: Penguin, 1967.

Hirsch, B. J. "Natural Support Systems and Coping with Major Life Changes". *American Journal of Community Psychology*, 1980, *8*, 159–72.

Holmes, T. H. and Rahe, R. H. "The Social Readjustment Rating Scale". *Journal of Psychosomatic Research*, 1967, *11*, 213–18.

Holmes, T. H. and Masuda, M. "Life Change and Illness Susceptibility". In B. S. Dohrenwend and B. P. Dohrenwend (Eds.), *Stressful Life Events*. New York: Wiley, 1973.

Hopson, B. "Transition: Understanding and Managing Personal Change". In D. Griffiths (Ed.), *Psychology and Medicine*. London: Macmillan, 1981.

Hunter, E. J. "The Prisoner of War: Coping with the Stress of Isolation". In R. H. Moos (Ed.), *Human Adaptation*. Lexington: Heath, 1976.

Ilfield, F. W. "Low Income and Psychiatric Symptomatology". Paper presented at meeting of the American Psychiatric Association, Toronto, 1977.

Jahoda, M. "The Impact of Unemployment in the 1930s and the 1970s". *Bulletin of the British Psychological Society*, 1979, *32*, 309–14.

Janis, I. L. "Psychodynamic Aspects of Stress Tolerance". In S. A. Klausner (Ed.), *The Quest for Self-control*. New York: The Free Press, 1965.

Janis, I. L. *Stress and Frustration*. New York: Harcourt, Brace, Jovanovich, 1971.

Janis, I. L. "Aftermath of the Atomic Disasters". In M. H. Moos (Ed.), *Human Adaptation*. Lexington: Heath, 1976.

Kellett, A. *Combat Motivation: The Behavior of Soldiers in Battle*. The Hague: Kluwer, Nijhoff, 1982.

Kirschenbaum, D. S. and Tomarken, A. J. "On Facing the Generalization Problem: The Study of Self-regulatory Failure". In P. C. Kendall

(Ed.), *Advances in Cognitive–Behavioral Research and Therapy*. New York: Academic Press, 1982.

Kohlberg, L., Yaeger, J. and Hjertholm, E. "Private Speech: Four Studies and a Review of Theories". *Child Development*, 1968, *39*, 691–736.

Langer, E., Janis, I. and Wolfer, J. "Reduction of Psychological Stress in Surgery Patients". *Journal of Experimental Social Psychology*, 1975, *1*, 155–66.

Lauer, R. H. and Lauer, J. C. "The Experience of Change: Tempo and Stress". In G. Zollschan and W. Hirsch (Eds.), *Social Change*. New York: Wiley, 1976.

Lazarus, A. A. "Toward an Egoless State of Being". In A. Ellis and R. Grieger (Eds.), *Handbook of Rational–Emotive Therapy*. New York: Springer, 1977.

Lazarus, R. S. *Patterns of Adjustment*. New York: McGraw–Hill, 1976.

Lazarus, R. S. and Cohen, J. B. "Environmental Stress". In I. Altman and J. F. Wohlwill (Eds.), *Human Behavior and Environment, Volume 2*. New York: Plenum, 1976.

Lefcourt, H. M. "Locus of Control and Coping with Life's Events". In E. Staub (Ed.), *Personality*. Englewood Cliffs, New Jersey: Prentice–Hall, 1980.

Levine, S. V. "Draft-dodgers: Coping with Stress, Adapting to Exile". In R. H. Moos (Ed.), *Human Adaptation*. Lexington: Heath, 1976.

Levinson, D. J., Darrow, C. M., Klein, E. B., Levinson, M. H. and Braxton, M. "The Psychosocial Development of Men in Early Adulthood and the Mid-life Crisis". In D. F. Ricks, A. Thomas, and M. Roff (Eds.), *Life History Research in Psychopathology*. Minneapolis: University of Minnesota Press, 1974.

Lockwood, D. "The Contribution of Sexual Harassment to Stress and Coping in Confinement". In N. Parisi (Ed.), *Coping with Imprisonment*. Beverly Hills, California: Sage, 1982.

Mahl, G. F. "Anxiety, HCl Secretion and Peptic Ulcer Etiology". *Psychosomatic Medicine*, 1949, *11*, 30–44.

Mahl, G. F. *Psychological Conflict and Defence*. New York: Harcourt, Brace, Jovanovich, 1971.

Marlatt, G. A. and Gordon, J. R. "Determinants of Relapse: Implications for the Maintenance of Behavior Change". In P. O. Davidson and S. M. Davidson (Eds.), *Behavioral Medicine: Changing Health Lifestyles*. New York: Brunner/Mazel, 1980.

Meichenbaum, D. *Cognitive Behavior Modification*. Morristown, New Jersey: General Learning Press, 1974.

Meichenbaum, D. "Enhancing Creativity by Modifying what Subjects Say to Themselves". *American Educational Research Journal*, 1975, *12*, 129–45.

Meichenbaum, D. *Cognitive–Behavior Modification*. New York: Plenum, 1977.

Milgram, S. "The Experience of Living in Cities". *Science*, 1970, *167*, 1461–8.

Miller, G. A., Galanter, E. and Pribram, K. H. *Plans and the Structure of Behavior*. New York: Holt, Rinehart and Winston, 1960.

Miller, S. M. "Why having Control Reduces Stress: If I can stop the roller coaster, I don't want to get off". In J. Garber and M. E. P. Seligman (Eds.), *Human Helplessness*. New York: Academic Press, 1980.

Moran, L. *The Anatomy of Courage*. London: Constable, 1966.

Myers, J. K., Lindenthal, J. J. and Pepper, M. P. "Social Class, Life Events, and Psychiatric Symptoms: A Longitudinal Study". In B. S. Dohrenwend and B. P. Dohrenwend (Eds.), *Stressful Life Events*. New York: Wiley, 1973.

Nardini, J. E. "Psychiatric Concepts of Prisoners of War Confinement". *Military Medicine*, 1962, *127*, 299–307.

Novaco, R. W. *Anger Control: The Development and Evaluation of an Experimental Treatment*. Lexington: Heath, 1975.

Ostwald, P. and Bittner, E. "Life Adjustment after Severe Persecution". In R. H. Moos (Ed.), *Human Adaptation*. Lexington: Heath, 1976.

Parkinson, L. and Rachman, S. "Are Intrusive Thoughts Subject to Habituation?" *Behavior Research and Therapy*, 1980, *18*, 409–18.

Pearlin, L. I. and Schooler, C. "The Structure of Coping". *Journal of Health and Social Behavior*, 1978, *19*, 2–21.

Pirsig, R. *Zen and the Art of Motorcycle Maintenance*. New York: William Morrow, 1974.

Prioleau, L., Murdock, M. and Brody, N. "An Analysis of Psychotherapy versus Placebo Studies". *The Behavioral and Brain Sciences*, 1983, *6*, 275–310.

Rasch, W. "The Effects of Indeterminate Detention". *International Journal of Law and Psychiatry*, 1981, *4*, 417–31.

Raush, H. L., Goodrich, W. and Campbell, J. D. "Adaptation to the First Years of Marriage". In R. H. Moos (Ed.), *Human Adaptation*. Lexington: Heath, 1976.

Rimm, D. C. and Masters, J. C. *Behavior Therapy*. New York: Academic Press, 1979.

Ruff, G. E. and Korchin, S. J. "Psychological Responses of the Mercury

Astronauts to Stress". In G. H. Grosser, H. Wechsler and M. Green-
blatt (Eds.), *The Threat of Impending Disaster*. Cambridge, Massa-
chusetts: MIT Press, 1964.

Sands, B. *My Shadow Ran Fast*. Englewood Cliffs, New Jersey:
Prentice–Hall, 1964.

Scheerer, M. "Problem Solving". *Scientific American*, 1963, *208*,
118–28.

Sears, R. R. "Experimental Studies of Projection, 1: Attribution of
Traits". *Journal of Social Psychology*, 1936, 7, 151–63.

Selye, H. "The Stress Concept Today". In I. L. Kutash, and L. B. Schle-
singer (Eds.), *Handbook on Stress and Anxiety*. San Francisco:
Jossey–Bass, 1980.

Shaffer, M. *Life after Stress*. New York: Plenum, 1982.

Shatan, C. F. "Stress Disorders among Viet-Nam Veterans: The
Emotional Content of Combat Continues". In C. R. Figley (Ed.), *Stress
Disorders among Viet-Nam Veterans*. New York: Bruner/Mazel,
1978.

Silver, R. L. and Wortman, C. B. "Coping with Undesirable Life Events".
In J. Garber and M.E.P. Seligman (Eds.), *Human Helplessness*. New
York: Academic Press, 1980.

Spaulding, R. C. and Ford, C. V. "The Pueblo Incident: Psychological
Reactions to the Stresses of Imprisonment and Repatriation". In R. H.
Moos (Ed.), *Human Adaptation*. Lexington: Heath, 1976.

Spivack, G., Platt, J. J. and Shure, M. B. *The Problem-solving Approach
to Adjustment*. San Francisco: Jossey–Bass, 1976.

Suinn, R. and Richardson, F. "Anxiety-management Training: A
Nonspecific Behavior Therapy Program for Anxiety Control".
Behavior Therapy, 1971, *2*, 498–510.

Sutherland, S. and Scherl, D. J. "Patterns of Response among Victims of
Rape". In R. H. Moos (Ed.), *Human Adaptation*. Lexington: Heath,
1976.

Trower, P., Bryant, B. and Argyle, M. *Social Skills and Mental Health*.
Pittsburgh: University of Pittsburgh Press, 1978.

Turk, D. C. "Cognitive-behavioral Techniques in the Management of
Pain". In J. P. Foreyt and D. J. Rathjen (Eds.), *Cognitive Behavior
Therapy*. New York: Plenum, 1978.

Walker, L. E. *The Battered Woman*. New York: Harper & Row, 1979.

Weiner, I. B. *Principles of Psychotherapy*. New York: Wiley, 1975.

Wellman, B. "Applying Network Analysis to the Study of Support". In
B. H. Gottlieb (Ed.), *Social Networks and Social Support*. Beverly
Hills, California: Sage, 1981.

Westermeyer, J. "Amok". In C. T. H. Friedmann and R. A. Faguet (Eds.), *Extraordinary Disorders of Human Behavior*. New York: Plenum, 1982.

Whitmore, J. R. *Giftedness, Conflict and Underachievement*. Boston: Allyn & Bacon, 1980.

Wiener, A., Gerber, I., Battin, D. and Arkin, A. M. "The Process and Phenomenology of Bereavement". In B. Schoenberg *et al.* (Eds.), *Bereavement*. New York: Columbia University Press, 1975.

Wilkinson, C. B. "Aftermath of a Disaster: The Collapse of the Hyatt Regency Hotel Skywalks". *American Journal of Psychiatry*, 1983, *140*, 1134–9.

Willerman, L. *The Psychology of Individual and Group Differences*. San Francisco: Freeman, 1979.

Wohlwill, J. F. "Human Adaptation to Levels of Environmental Stimulation". *Human Ecology*, 1974, *2*, 127–47.

Zilbergeld, B. *The Shrinking of America*. Boston: Little, Brown, 1983.

Acknowledgements

The author would like to thank the following copyright holders for their permission to use material which appears on the following pages.

Pages 37–8: Dubos, R. *Man Adapting*. New Haven: Yale University Press, 1965. Copyright Yale University Press, 1965.

Page 38: Milgram, S. "The Experience of Living in Cities". *Science*, vol. 167, pp 1461–8, 13 March 1970. Copyright 1970 by the American Association for the Advancement of Science.

Pages 43–44: Table 1. Reprinted with permission from *Journal of Psychosomatic Research, 11*, T. H. Holmes and R. H. Rahe, "The Social Readjustment Rating Scale", Copyright 1967, Pergamon Press Ltd. Reprinted with permission from Pergamon Press and T. H. Holmes.

Pages 52, 54: Table 2. From Levinson, D. J., Darrow, C. M., Klein, E. B., Levinson, M. H. and Braxton, M. "The Psychosocial Development of Men in Early Adulthood and the Mid-life Crisis". In D. F. Hicks, A. Thomas and M. Roff (Eds.), *Life History Research in Psychopathology*. Minneapolis: University of Minnesota Press, 1974. Copyright 1974 by University of Minnesota Press.

Page 59: Crisp, R. *Brazen Chariots*. New York: Norton, 1959. Copyright 1959 (British Commonwealth) Frederick Muller Ltd. Copyright (USA and elsewhere) W. W. Norton & Company, Inc.

Page 61: Collins, W. R. F. "Nazi Mentality". *American Journal of Psychiatry*, 1945, *102*, 131–2. Copyright 1945, by the American Psychiatric Association.

Pages 62–3, 151: Dimsdale, J. E. "The Coping Behavior of Nazi Concentration Camp Survivors". *American Journal of Psychiatry*, 1974, *131*, 792–7. Copyright 1974 by the American Psychiatric Association.

Page 65: Janis, I. L. "Psychodynamic Aspects of Stress Tolerance". In S. A. Klausner (Ed.), *The Quest for Self-control.* New York: The Free Press, 1965. Copyright © 1965 by The Free Press, a division of the Macmillan Company.

Page 67: Walker, L. E. *The Battered Woman.* New York: Harper & Row, 1979. Copyright Lenore Walker. Permission granted by Mary Yost Associates Inc., 59 East 54th St., New York, NY 10022.

Page 69: Hunter, E. J. "The Prisoner of War: Coping with the Stress of Isolation". In R. H. Moos (Ed.), *Human Adaptation.* Lexington: Heath, 1976. Copyright D. C. Heath and Company, 1976.

Page 70: From the book, *My Shadow Ran Fast* by Bill Sands. Copyright 1964 by Prentice-Hall, Inc.

Page 72: Cohen S. and Taylor L. *Psychological Survival: The Experience of Long-term Imprisonment.* Harmondsworth: Penguin, 1972. Copyright 1972 by Penguin Books.

Page 90: Hamburg, D. A., Hamburg, B. and DeGoza, S. "Adaptive Problems and Mechanisms in Severely Burned Patients". *Psychiatry*, 1953, *16*, 1–20. Copyright 1953 by *Psychiatry.*

Pages 96–7: Hinkle, L. E. "The Effect of Exposure to Culture Change, Social Change and Changes in Interpersonal Relationships on Health". In B. S. Dohrenwend and B. P. Dohrenwend (Eds.), *Stressful Life Events: Their Nature and Effects.* New York: Wiley, 1973. Copyright 1973 by John Wiley & Sons, Inc.

Pages 116, 144–7: Table 3. Rimm, D. C. and Masters, J. C. *Behavior Therapy.* New York: Academic Press, 1979. Copyright 1979 by Academic Press. Reprinted by permission of Academic Press and J. C. Masters.

Page 127: Bernheim, H. *Hypnosis and Suggestion.* New Hyde Park: University Books, 1964. Copyright 1964 by Lyle Stuart, Inc.

Page 129: Kohlberg, L., Yaeger, J. and Hjertholm, E. "Private Speech: Four Studies and a Review of Theories". *Child Development*, 1968, *39*, 691–736. Copyright 1968 by The Society for Research in Child Development, Inc.

Page 131: Table 4. From D. Meichenbaum. *Cognitive Behavior Modification.* Morristown; General Learning Press, 1974.

Index